How to
Custom Paint &
Graphics

by Jon Kosmoski and Timothy Remus

Published by:
Wolfgang Inc.
P.O. Box 10
Scandia, MN 55073

First published in 1997 by Wolfgang Publications Inc., P.O. Box 10, Scandia, MN 55073, USA.

© Timothy Remus, 1997

ISBN number: 0-9641358-5-X

Printed and bound in the USA

On the Cover:

The Chevy Tahoe with the wild graphics was painted at Let's Get Graphic in Spring Lake Park, Minnesota while the furling flag is the work of Nancy Brooks in Hanover, Massachusetts

How To:

Custom Paint & Graphics

Contents

Acknowledgments

A variety of artists helped with this new Graphics text, without them this book wouldn't exist. In alphabetical order we wish to begin our thanks with Andy Anderson from Anderson Studios in Nashville, Tennessee. Andy is able to somehow combine every color in the rainbow into one motorcycle paint scheme and still have the whole thing turn out tasteful rather than garish.

Bruce Bush from Wizard Custom Studios in Ham Lake, Minnesota paints everything from street rods and tail-dragging leadsleds to hot Harley-Davidsons, often with design help from motorhead and artist, Ken Madden.

Nancy Brooks of Brooks Sign, located outside Boston, Massachusetts, applies her wonderful mix of detail, design and color to everything from semi-trailers to motorcycles and local promotional vehicles.

Let's Get Graphic in Spring Lake Park Minnesota is a good example of new math: when one + one + one = four. That is to say the talents of Brian Gall, Leah Begin and Lenni Hubbard combine in a synergistic fashion to create a team capable of doing nearly any type of paint or graphic work.

Lenni Schwartz from Krazy Kolors in North St. Paul, Minnesota is equally at home with a paint brush, pinstripe brush or airbrush, and often combines all three into his unique and Krazy designs.

Last only by virtue of his last name, Jeremy Vecoli, from Minneapolis, Minnesota started with a simple airbrush and a video tape and ended up teaching airbrush painting at a local technical College.

To one and all we can only say thanks: For letting us into the shop, for having the patience to wait while we re-loaded film in the camera, and for proof reading various parts of the manuscript. To Andy and Jeremy we have to add an addition word of gratitude for supplying material that could be used directly in the book.

Introduction

Art on a moving canvas

It all started a few years back when Jon Kosmoski and I agreed to publish the fourth edition of his Kustom Painting Secrets book. That book covers mostly custom painting on complete vehicles, and though it provides a wealth of information there just wasn't room to include extensive information on airbrushing, or the layout of an elaborate graphic.

Thus was born the idea of a Custom Paint and Graphics book. When it comes to learning a particular skill the best information usually comes from people who already in the trade. This book brings you a variety of painting and graphic painting sequences, all done with experienced and well known artists. The sequences run the gamut from layout to pinstriping, from airbrushing to brushing by hand. Though there is plenty of text, there is also an abundance of photos. What you might call Show & Tell with the emphasis on the Show.

The techniques covered here include some very traditional brush work as well as the most modern airbrush applications. The designs too include both the simple and the complex, the classics and the cutting-edge.

The work covered includes both simple and complex layouts and paint jobs. From scallops laid out over an existing paint job, to a set of graphics

Jon Kosmoski's
Kustom Painting Secrets
HOW TO PAINT YOUR:
CAR · MOTORCYCLE · TRUCK · STREET ROD

Learn From The Master How To:
• Use Plastic Filler
• Prepare For Paint
• Shoot Kandies & Pearls
• Do a Basecoat-Clearcoat Paint Job
• Do Flames, Tapeouts & Artwork
• Apply a Marble Paint Job

30 YEARS OF TRICKS & TECHNIQUES
BY JON KOSMOSKI

so complex they become the paint job.

More than half this book is printed in color, simply because the sequences are so bright and beautiful it wouldn't be right to present them any other way.

Chapter One

Shop Tools, Equipment and Safety

Shop Necessities

The operation of even a small shop requires the right equipment. That list of tools includes the airbrush or spray gun, a compressor to drive it, possibly a computer for cutting masks, hand brushes for additional work and the right safety equipment so all the work can be done without damage to you or the environment.

This chapter discusses the pros and cons of various airbrush, spray gun and compressor designs - which ultimately must be tied to your

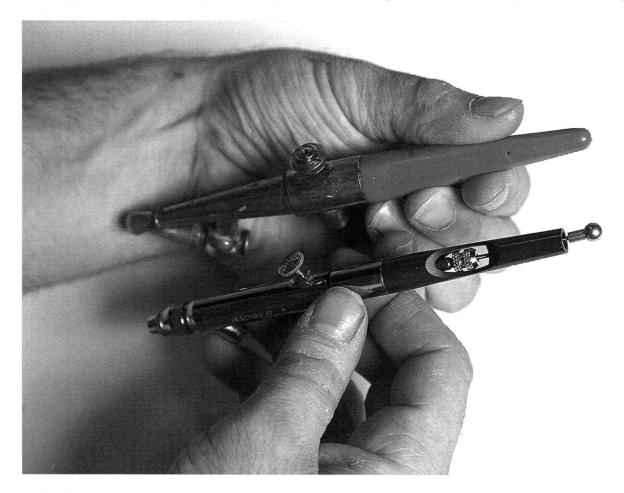

Airbrushes, no matter which brand, come in two basic styles. Single stage airbrushes like that in the background use the trigger only to control the air, control of the material is done externally. Double stage airbrushes like that in the front, use to trigger to control both the air and the material moving through the airbrush.

budget and usage. More and more graphic artists are using computers in their shops and we provide a look at the system requirements for anyone considering such a purchase.

A safety section is included here as well. We sincerely hope you will take the time to read and consider the warnings and suggestions. The new paints are better than ever but they require intelligent, careful handling by intelligent, careful artists like you.

AIRBRUSHES

Airbrushes come in a variety of shapes manufactured from metal, plastic or a combination of the two. Prices vary considerably for what is often very similar equipment. There are a number of quality airbrush manufacturers out there and it seems that each artist has his or her favorite brand. This is another case where finding the right equipment means matching your needs and budget to the available airbrushes and accessories on the market.

Airbrushes break down into two basic designs, single or double-action. Single-action means that the trigger only does one thing, control the air leaving the gun. With a single-action airbrush the amount of paint moving through the brush is controlled with an external adjustment. A double-action airbrush on the other hand uses the trigger to control both the air and the material moving through the brush.

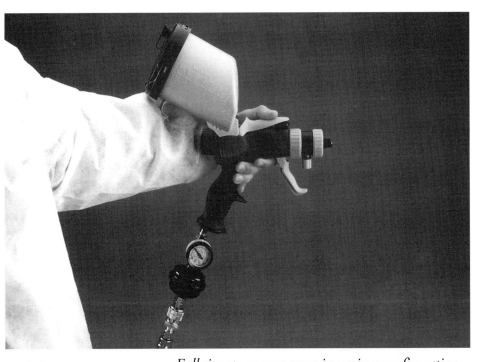

Full size spray guns come in various configurations including HVLP guns (High Volume, Low Pressure) like this OMX model from DeVilbiss. By reducing the pressure of the airstream leaving the gun these guns offer much-improved transfer efficiencies.

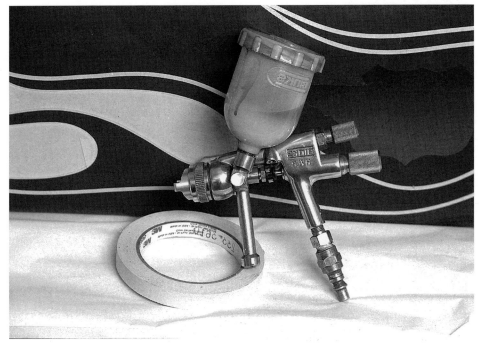

Larger than an airbrush but smaller than a full-sized gun, touch up spray guns like this gravity feed HVLP model from Binks offer a good alternative for small areas.

Though the folks as Paasche Air Brush recommend the single-action for beginners, anyone doing Graphics work on vehicles will eventually need a double-action airbrush. Most of these units control the air with an up and down movement of the trigger, and the material with a back and forth movement of the same trigger. This allows one brush to go from a fat half-inch line to a pencil thin shadow in about one second. All without stopping

There are a tremendous number of airbrushes available. On the left, top to bottom are a Thayer & Chandler Vega 2000, an Iwata Eclipse and a Paasche H. On the right is a Badger 360, a Badger Anthem, a Badger Crescendo and a Sonar 20-20.

Full time airbrush artists often have racks of brushes and paint jars so changing guns or colors is as simple as possible. All the airbrushes are attached to one manifold and driven by the same compressor.

to adjust any external controls or change needles and tips.

Though different artists disagree as to the brand of airbrush they prefer, they do agree that what makes a good airbrush for the type of work covered in this book is range. As Lenni Schwartz from Krazy Kolors explains, "It's nice to have a gun with a lot of range so you don't have to change the needles to go from a fat to a skinny line." Jeremy Vecoli adds in Chapter Three that airbrushes with a broad range of spraying abilities are somewhat new to the market so again you need to inquire as to the abilities of each gun.

Most airbrushes can be equipped with different needle and tip combinations, primarily to handle different viscosity paints. Automotive paint falls between the extremes of illustrator's ink and thick ceramic materials, so you probably want to buy the airbrush with the mid-sized tip and needle. Andy Anderson adds the comment that, "The tips, especially in double-action airbrushes, must be perfectly straight.

In addition to range you want an airbrush that will handle automotive paints and solvents without any internal damage - most will, but it's always best to ask before buying.

Working on vehicles usually means applying a relatively large amount of paint and for this reason an airbrush designed to accept a jar of paint, as opposed to a small thimble-sized container, is a better choice. This also allows the user to set up a series of jars with all the necessary colors before beginning the job. Some of the new guns will accept either jars or the small paint cups.

Though the manufacturers recommend running their guns at 15 to 40 pounds, there are a number of artists using shop air, at roughly 100 psi unregulated. What the manufacturers do agree on is the need to keep the equipment clean, clean, clean.

CONVENTIONAL SPRAY GUNS

Though the emphasis of this book is on Graphics, which call for the use of (primarily) airbrushes, we though it best to touch on the different types of conventional spray guns available today.

Spray guns, whether full-sized or touch up models, come in two basic designs with variations on each. The standard siphon (or high-pressure gun) has been around since the turn of the century and is now joined by the newer HVLP gun (high volume low pressure).

The high-pressure guns

Full size spray guns typically have two controls, air to the horns and material. Though other configurations are offered, the two-knob layout shown here is somewhat standard: The upper knob controls air to the horns and the shape of the fan, the lower knob controls the material.

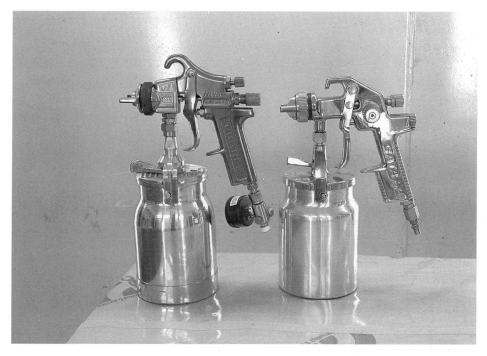

HVLP and standard high-pressure spray guns are hard to tell apart. The gun on the left is an HVLP from Sharpe, on the right is a high-pressure gun from Sata. Nearly all full size guns use a double-action trigger which controls both the air and the material.

are known for good atomization. The high speed air stream (usually forty psi or more) does a good job of breaking up the paint and delivering it to the object being painted. Yet some of that paint misses the object entirely and some hits with such force that it bounces back off into the air. Standard siphon style guns get as little as 25 percent of the paint on the car. The rest of the paint and solvents go up in the air or out with the exhaust.

Transfer efficiency is a measure of the amount of paint that actually makes it from the gun to the object. Siphon style guns have a transfer efficiency of only about 25 percent while the new HVLP guns achieve efficiencies of 75 percent and more.

HVLP guns and systems atomize the paint with a high volume of low pressure air instead of the standard high-pressure siphon-type gun where a small volume of high-pressure air is used to atomize the paint.

By delivering roughly three times as much material to the object the amount of paint used is reduced. This means lower material costs, less overspray and less solvent usage meaning reduced VOCs in the atmosphere. It also means the fog in the paint booth is greatly reduced.

Most of the new HVLP guns convert the high-pressure compressor air to a low pressure air with more volume. The air leaving the gun measures less than ten psi. Some of these guns pressurize the paint in the pot and use that pressure to bring the paint up to meet the air stream.

HVLP guns tend to cost more than comparable high-pressure siphon guns. The HVLP equipment makes more sense when you consider the fact that this system will use less paint and create less overspray. Most HVLP systems will create less than half the overspray meaning less chance to

Computers can be used for more than just cutting vinyl graphics for the sides of conversion vans and 4X4s. A computer of only moderate capacity can be used as a design tool, and to drive the plotter/cutter that cuts the masks you used to cut by hand.

breathe the often toxic fumes and less clean up in the shop afterwards. The better examples make candy painting easier due to their fine paint atomization.

COMPRESSORS

If you're in a shop that does conventional spray painting work you can simply tie into the shop air and skip the compressor purchase altogether. What you do need is a regulator to regulate the shop's high-pressure air down to a more reasonable figure needed by most airbrushes.

Compressors designed to run airbrushes include small diaphragm units, the quiet models that use an Air conditioning type compressor, and even mini-tank type units intended to run more than one airbrush. You can even power the airbrush off small propellant cans or a larger bottle of carbon dioxide or nitrogen.

If space and/or portability is a requirement then you need one of the small compressors designed for airbrush work. A small "shop" type compressor of about 1 horsepower is probably a better value in terms of air-per-dollar, though they are admittedly much larger. Remember that if you intend to run touch up guns or conventional spray guns you need at least three and possibly a five horsepower compressor.

Anyone who opts for the small "airbrush" compressor should listen to one run before they buy. Some of these make as much noise as a Harley with drag pipes. The other consideration is the CFM (cubic feet per minute) capacity, which is quite limited in the case of some small compressors.

No matter which unit you buy be sure to put a moisture trap on the air hose and if the unit has a tank make it a habit to drain the tank on a regular basis.

This group of brushes is meant to be used with water based paints and includes numbers 0, 2,6,8 and 10 from left to right, and 3/8, 1/2 and 5/8 inch flats on the right. These should be stored dry.

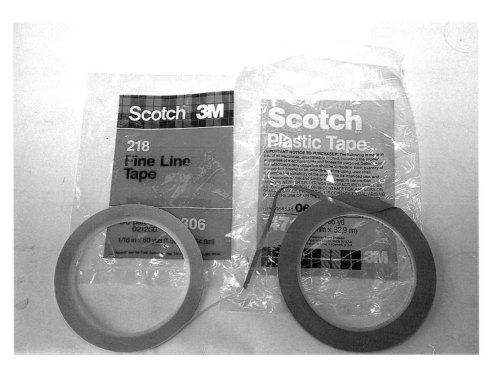

Plastic tapes like these from 3M are a handy masking tool, as they will stretch without tearing more readily than will conventional masking tape.

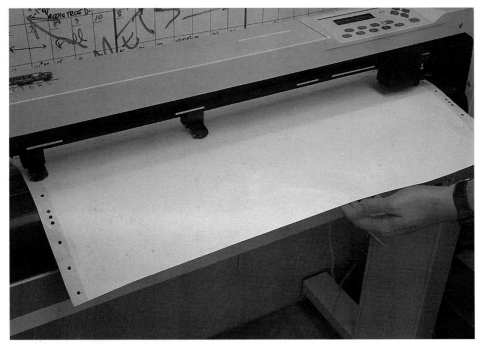

Vinyl cutters like this are driven by your computer and used to cut the Gerbermask or other vinyl masking material. No matter how you feel about computers, this is much faster than doing it by hand. And each copy is just that, an exact copy.

BRUSHES

Many people assume that Graphics applied to a car, truck or motorcycle are done with airbrushes. Yet the well-rounded artist is able to mix airbrushing with hand lettering and striping. The tools of this trade are pretty basic. Which is not to say you can just run down to the hardware store, buy some small paint brushes and start painting signs and race cars.

Brushes break down into groups, each one designed to perform a particular job. In addition to the various sizes, brushes come in both natural and synthetic bristles of various lengths. Before buying a brush or group of brushes you need to know the surface you will be painting on, the type of work you intend to do and the chemistry of the paint that will be used. What follows is a brief introduction to the most common brush types. Additional information on brushes, lettering and pinstriping can be found in Chapter Three.

BRUSH TYPES AND USAGE:

Stripping brushes: These specialized brushes with the short handle and long bristles are designed to hold enough paint so you can lay down a long line without having to go back every two inches and re-load the paint brush. Available in both natural squirrel hair and synthetics, these brushes are rated numerically, from 00 to 5, with 00 being the smallest and 5 the biggest.

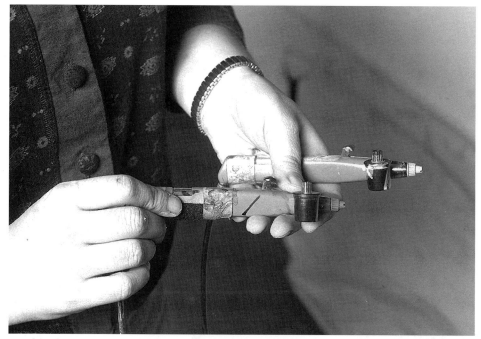

Airbrushes come in a wide variety of shapes, made from both metal and plastic. These plastic brushes are from Aztek and have the advantage of being very light in weight.

Note, for more on brushes see Chapter Three.

Showcard brushes: These are lettering brushes with red sable bristles available in a variety of sizes. Many painters use these with water-based paint when painting on posters.

Fitches: Probably not ideal for anyone applying Graphics to cars, trucks or motorcycles, these lettering brushes are good for work on rough textured surfaces.

White bristle cutters: Meant for sign work that requires painting relatively large areas, the brushes look like mini house brushes and come in sizes from one to three inches.

Lettering quills: These brushes work for many applications and are a good staple brush for anyone doing sign work, whether those signs are attached to a wall or part of a vehicle. Both grey and brown squirrel hair are available with brown being the softer of the two.

Ox hair truck lettering quills: These flat square ended lettering brushes are good for large letters or filling in the center of a large area. They can also be used to apply the sizing used with gold leaf.

MASKING TAPE AND SPECIAL TAPE PRODUCTS

Masking tape comes in everything from 2 inch wide rolls to 1/16th inch wide plastic or fine-line tape. In addition some specialized multi-stripe tapes are available for pinstriping use (more on this tape in Chapter Three). The most important thing to remember about masking tape is to buy brand name tape from an auto parts store or paint jobber. All masking tape is not created equal.

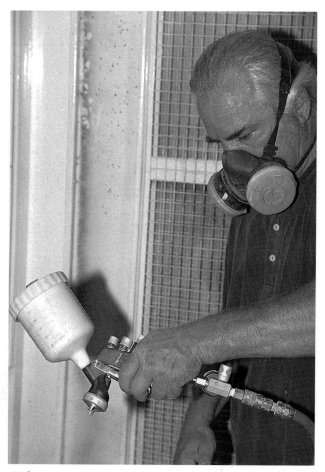

When spraying any paint material it is necessary to wear a TC-23 style charcoal respirator. Spraying catalyzed kandys and clears requires a full fresh-air hood with it's own air supply.

A sign-painter's tool box, complete with lettering quills and striping brushes on the left, more quills and a flat on the right.

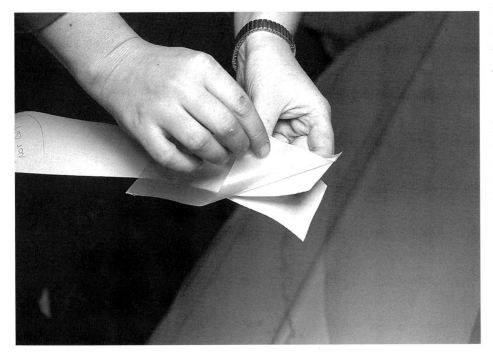

Here you can see what we call the "three layer sandwich" of masking material made up of: the wax paper that backs the vinyl, the vinyl itself and the transfer paper used to "transfer" the vinyl onto the vehicle.

Some is meant for home use and some just isn't very good. Don't use the cheap tape from the discount store or you risk tearing off the original paint when you pull off the tape.

COMPUTERS AND CUTTERS

Computers are pretty hard to ignore these days, whether you're talking about a small business or a graphics layout. Computer cut and generated vinyl graphics, so common on trucks and vans these days, is *not* what this book is about. That is not to say, however, that a computer and vinyl cutter have no place in a Graphics shop. As illustrated in Chapter Four the computer and cutter can be used to cut the masking vinyl. Which means you can take the original sketch, scan it into the computer, enlarge or modify it, and then use the cutter, instead of your X-Acto knife, to cut the vinyl mask.

Not only does this save you the time needed to cut out the mask, it means the mask for the other side of the vehicle can be created with only a few keystrokes. It also means the second mask is a perfect duplicate of the first.

Magazines like *AutoGraphics* are filled with ads for computers, software and plotter/cutter/printers. All this can be fairly intimidating for the non-nerd. To help the first-time buyer get the most for their computer dollar we asked Rory Bedell, owner of l.i.n.e. Company for a little buyer's advice. Rory sells to both the Sign and Graphics industries and understands both real-world budgets and the need to make the buying decision as simple as possible.

At the heart of this decision is the computer and though Rory is a Macintosh dealer she says you can easily use either a Mac or a Windows/PC machine. She explains that though the requirements vary with the brand, "You don't need a real expensive machine, a lot of people have a computer at home or for the business that could be used for this. But you do need at least 16 megabytes of RAM (random access memory) if it's a Mac and 32 megs if it's a PC machine. I don't know why the PCs need more RAM to operate the Graphics software, but they do. The computer should also have a math co-processor and a hard drive with at least 500 megabytes of storage."

The computer drives the vinyl cutter and of course the cutters come in a whole host of sizes and capabilities. Fifteen inch wide cutters are probably the smallest that a Sign or Graphics shop should consider. "Your better bet is a 24 inch cutter," says Rory. "They're still inexpensive yet big enough to do anything from motorcycle tanks to trucks. With bigger jobs you will have to use more than one piece of vinyl, which means you have to be sure the register is correct where they meet, but you can easily do that."

Without some good software all that expensive hardware isn't worth a damn. For beginners Rory likes the software package: Corel Draw, which works well on either Macs or PCs. For more sophisticated work Amiable Technology makes a program called FlexiSign, one of Rory's favorites, which comes in various levels. Though some graphics supply companies have their own software Rory likes to use the more universal programs, "Some software will only work with one company's cutter for example, so then you're much more limited. There must be at least 20 software programs, in addition to the two I mentioned, that will work fine and don't tie you to one brand of hardware."

A scanner makes it easy to take a sketch or photo and use that as the basis for a design. Like everything else these come in everything from the four-cylinder econo-box model to the full-boat Cadillac version with air conditioning and 10-speaker stereo. Though the stereo in the Cadillac might sound good, this is a case where more money won't get you more performance. The high-end scanners are good for color work, but all you want to do in this case is scan in your designs. Rory suggests that a simple two-hundred dollar

This Nancy Brooks design is a good example of the detail that is possible with an airbrush. Note the horse, their harnesses and the little clouds of dust (which evoke speed) coming off each of the hooves.

Jar-fed airbrushes like these from Thayer & Chandler hold more material for bigger jobs and also offer the artist the opportunity to fill a group of jars with various colors before the job starts.

Some of the best designs involve both airbrushing and hand lettering. Lenni Schwartz is able to take and complete a wider variety of work because of his wide ranging talents.

scanner will do all you really need.

Once you've got the equipment it's pretty easy to get started. "Most of the people I sell a package to are up and running, doing simple designs and signs, within the first day," promises Rory. "The tutorials that come with the software packages are pretty good, all it really takes is time, patience and practice."

SAFETY

We see plenty of airbrush artists who paint without any respirators. They seem to feel that because they are using such small amounts of materials the effects are negligible. Yet, these materials are toxic even in small doses and they will accumulate in your body.

For painting with non-catalyzed paints you need a TC23, which is basically a double-charcoal respirator. Be sure to replace both the pre-filters and the charcoal canisters as recommended by the manufacturer. You've only got one set of lungs and you must protect them at all times even when using relatively small amounts of material.

The most toxic of the new paint materials are the isocyanates used to catalyze modern urethane paints (See Chapter Two for more on the various paints). When painting with isocyanates, or even when pouring and mixing the material, you need to use a TC19C, which is an air supply hood. One of the major places toxic fumes enter your body is through the mucous membranes around your eyes. So if the mask doesn't cover your eyes you need goggles or safely glasses that fit tight around the eyes.

With our House of Kolor products the basecoats are not catalyzed so you are not exposed to these chemicals unless you're spraying urethane kandys or clearcoats. For this reason many small shops do most of their painting with our Shimrin family of basecoat paints and then take the parts to a facility with a paint booth for the application of the clearcoats.

If you're doing more than just airbrush work in a small area a painter's suit is a good idea, especially if you're working with catalyzed material. The suit will also prevent lint on your clothes from falling into the paint. The Jon Kosmoski book: *Kustom Painting Secrets*, contains more information on safety as it relates to a typical booth environment and complete vehicle paint jobs.

Your skin is receptive and porous so you shouldn't get your hands into these materials. This is another good reason to wear gloves and a protective suit, and avoid the use of thinner to wash your hands.

As was mentioned in the *Kustom Painting Secrets* book, we recommend taking 400 units of Vitamin E every day as a preventive measure. The vitamin E takes the free radicals that might get in your system and puts them in the body's waste chain so they don't get lodged in your organs.

Extended kneeling on the concrete, as when you're working along the side of a car or truck, will ruin the cartilage in your knees. Use an insulator or knee pads between your knees and the floor or work from a small stool.

FLAMMABLE AND
TOXIC LIQUIDS

The care and handling of flammable liquids in your shop should be carefully considered. Specialized containers and cabinets for your flammables are available and they're a good idea. You want to keep children away from those materials if your shop is at home. You should have a flamma-

ble storage cabinet, it's an important piece of your plan for shop safety.

You need to have the proper type of storage and disposal for your waste thinners and paints. Many small shops have the toxic liquids and left over paint picked up by an approved toxic waste handling company. That way they are safely reclaimed or put into some form of retrieval unit. Be sure to follow the regulations for your shop and your part of the country.

How you're heating your shop is a critical issue. The fumes in the shop are both flammable and capable of traveling to an ignition source like the pilot light on the water heater or the wood burning stove.

You also need to have a number of good fire extinguishers designed for flammable liquids. I like Halon, but in a closed space you can't use Halon

Not everyone uses a computer-driven cutter to cut the masking vinyl. Nancy Brooks still cuts out all her materials with only an X-Acto knife.

because it robs the room of oxygen. The other common type is charged CO_2, an inert powder that blankets the fire.

Be careful with smoking substances. Have an area set aside for smoking and make sure that any cigarettes are put completely out. We always think "it can't happen here," but it can and it will if you don't work to create a safe shop environment.

INTERVIEW: BRIAN PETTERSEN, PAASCHE AIR BRUSH CO., CHICAGO, IL

Brian, to start with why don't you give me some history on Paasche.

My great grandfather Paasche came down from Norway right before the turn of the century and he started Paasche up in 1904, and we've been Paasche Airbrush ever since. He was a genius. He made all the brushes. Most of the brushes, the VL, the H air, are 30-40-50 years old, and they haven't changed too much over time.

So the basic designs were good enough that they're still being manufactured?

It's not too technological a product. It's not like the computer where it's advancing every year. There are small improvements we make year by year, but for the most part all of the airbrushes have been standard for quite a while. They'll change.

Your guns have a reputation for being very durable? What makes yours durable? What makes them unique?

The parts are chrome plated brass or stainless steel. There's a couple of washers in there, one's Teflon and the other is a plastic, they don't get affected by the paints. But there are no moving parts made from plastic so the airbrushes last. The H airbrush is the workhorse. People have had those for 20 years. At shows they'll come up to me and after 20 years they'll replace the tip and the

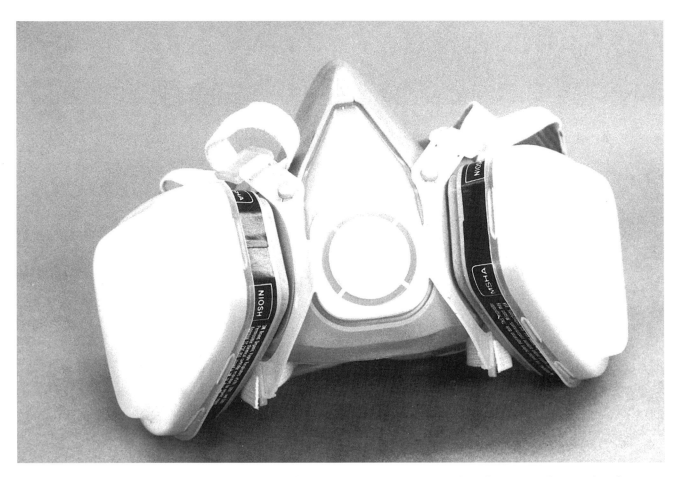

A dual cartridge charcoal respirator is adequate for most painting situations that do not involve catalyzed paints - though you should read the safety and technical information for each paint product.

18

needle, because they've dropped it or it's worn after time. They can last you forever if you take care of them.

The thrust of this book is graphics on motorcycles, trucks and automobiles. In that kind of situation, what do I want to look for in an airbrush?

First you have to decide what kind of control you need. The single-action trigger is more of a basic gun for backgrounds. If you want to get into the fine detail where you're fluctuating your pattern like on your motorcycles, you want to get the double-action VL model.

Maybe you could talk about single and double-action?

With the single-action brush you control the air with your trigger finger. The paint is controlled in the front with the tip, by opening and closing it. With the VL, with the double-action trigger, you push down on the trigger to get your air and then you pull the trigger back to control the paint flow. So you can control air and paint with one finger. You get more fine control of the lines and the patterns.

So now back to what do I want for doing car and motorcycle work?

Most people actually have the VL. The VL has a feature where you can roll back the needle and set it at a level so it kind of acts as a single-action.

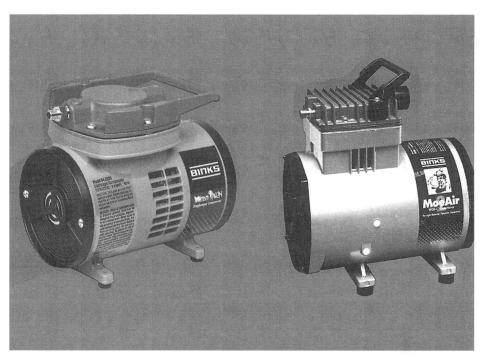

Compressors designed for airbrushes come in various styles. Binks offers both the simple pancake design and the silent "wobble-plate" models.

The best Graphic designs rely on illusion for much of their effect. In this Nancy Brooks image the dark holes become eye sockets, a trail of white becomes smoke or mist. Lettering was done by hand.

But it is a double action?

It is a double-action, but it can be kind of used as both. The one disadvantage on the double-action is that they're internal mix, and it's not as easy to clean. There are more moving parts. The single-action just has the tip and needle mounted on the outside. On the H model there are no internal parts. It's just the air valve and the tip and the needle where the bottle attaches, so it's very easy to clean. When you go to the VL (the most popu-

Inside most airbrushes, including those from Paasche you find mostly brass components which are often chrome plated before final assembly.

lar, it's the one everyone wants), it's all internally mixed whereas the single-action is external. The VL is definitely the most popular model. It's also closer to a regular big production spray gun in the way it works.

How important is the air supply for quality airbrush work?

You probably don't need more than 30 pounds of pressure, depending on the consistency of the material. You can run anywhere from 20 up to 50 pounds. Tee-shirt artists like to use 50 because it penetrates the fabric more readily. If you have a heavier paint material increasing air pressure helps to push it through the gun and atomize it properly too. On light materials you want to keep the pressure low, because you don't want it runny when it hits your project. That's the main problem people have. They're using the wrong consistency paint or the wrong pressure.

What about quality in terms of oil or water particles in the air supply?

Humidity is probably the biggest problem, because it will cause the gun to spit. Most people will put a moisture trap on their regulator or they can install an air hose that will take out most of

Hardly a computerized plant, airbrushes from Paasche are still built and assembled largely by hand.

the moisture. Like in the Midwest, it's really humid, or down South, you'll have to have something to control the moisture.

Is there any problem with running these off of a shop compressor, as long as you control the pressure?

No. A lot of people do. A lot of shops use airbrushes. They'll have a set up with 20 airbrushes for painting the products, and they'll run it off the shop air as long as they can regulate it down to 30 pounds or around there.

You talked a little bit about spitting, and I hear a lot of people complain about spitting. It seems to be an attribute of airbrushes, or at least some airbrushes. Tell me about spitting and what causes it and what people can do to avoid it.

There are paints bottled specifically for airbrush use and they'll either tell you how to thin it properly or they're already mixed for you. You want to have a milky or creamy consistency for the best effects. Most people have the problem where they're not getting any paint coming out, where it's spitting, and usually it's because the paint is too thick to be siphoned up the pick-up tube and then atomize as it leaves the gun. So it'll spit because it's pulling up air and the paint. That's probably the biggest problem we have when people call in. So it's not the gun, people don't read their material and they don't know to thin or to mix the paint right.

Do people have trouble because they don't keep the equipment clean?

A lot of people will use a brush once and then will send it back saying it's broken. Then we'll get it and it'll be clogged full of paint. That's probably the most important thing. Keep it clean and you won't have the problems.

What are the mistakes people (beginners especially) make?

Besides the paint, a lot of people will take the airbrush apart to clean it and when they're tightening the fixtures they won't use the wrench, which can create a variety of problems.

You have different sizes?

Different sizes mostly for the thicker paints. It also affects your pattern somewhat. With size 1 you'll get a finer line. Size 3 seems to be the most

popular for T-shirt artists. It will handle the medium consistency paints and give you a fine line too.

Automotive-type paint is going to higher solids content. Is that a problem for the airbrush user?

Most of them use the size 5 just because it has the largest tip orifice for the solids. A lot of people strain the paint to get the biggest particles out, because those will clog the brush. That's the biggest problem when they go to the high solids paints where they'll clog very easily.

Any final words of wisdom for people who are going to buy and use an airbrush for the first time?

If you're a beginner it's sometimes easier to start with a single-action. A lot of people graduate later to the double action. I would get a video or a book and spend time reading through the instructions that come with the airbrush. Before buying I would call someone who is knowledgeable to see what airbrush best suits your project.

Descended from a long line of airbrush manufacturers, Brian Pettersen is one of the hands-on managers at Paasche Airbrush.

Chapter Two

Paint and Materials

Urethanes, Lacquers, Enamel and More

To be a good custom and graphics painter you need complete control of your equipment and materials. Our House of Kolor paints are better than they've ever been, with more colors and better durability than ever before. But to get the full advantage of these materials you must understand each one: what it is and how to best mix and apply it. In this way you will get the most from our products (or any company's products). Remember that tech sheets, with additional infor-

Buffing is an option for most clearcoats. How many coats of clear should be applied and when is the best time to polish all depend on which clearcoat is used.

mation, are offered on all our products.

Though we've tried to make our paints as easy to use as possible, there isn't anything made that somebody can't foul up by not paying attention, or understanding the procedures required to do the work.

WHAT IT IS

Paint is made up of three basic components: pigment, resin and solvent, as well as a few additives.

Pigment is the material that gives the paint it's color. Though older paints often used lead-based pigments all the modern paints from House of Kolor have been converted to non-lead pigments. Resin (also known as binder) helps to hold the pigments together and keep them sticking to the metal. Solvent is the carrier used to make the paint thin enough to spray. In the case of lacquers a true thinner is used, while in the case of an enamel the solvent is called a reducer.

Additives are materials added to the paint to give it a certain property or help it overcome a problem much the way that additives are incorporated into modern oils to improve their performance.

Going back to the three basic components of paint, the solvent (a volatile material) evaporates (or oxidizes) after the paint is sprayed leaving behind the pigment and binder, known as the solids. Solvents that evaporate into the atmosphere are known in the industry as VOCs and have come under government regulation in many areas.

DIFFERENT FAMILIES OF PAINT

Automotive paints can be classified as either a lacquer, an enamel or a urethane. At House of Kolor we manufacture both urethane and lacquer based products. Our Shimrin basecoats can be topcoated with either lacquer or urethane kandies and clears (though mixing instructions are different depending on how they will be topcoated). These Shimrins are actually a unique combination of acrylic urethane and copolymers that behave like lacquer but far surpass lacquer in lasting performance.

LACQUER

Lacquer paints have been available for years

and years. During the 1950s, we painted hundreds of custom cars and bikes with lacquer, nitrocellulose lacquer to be exact. Today we offer acrylic lacquer for painters who need a lacquer-based product.

Custom painters have always liked lacquer because of it's fast drying times, low toxicity, great color and the ease with which spot repairs can be made. Custom painters often put lacquer on in multiple coats, wet sanding between coats. The end result is that classic deep shine.

The trouble with modern acrylic lacquer is it's lack of durability when compared to the urethanes and the large amount of maintenance a lacquer paint job requires. The other problem with lacquer paints is the VOC issue. The evaporating thinner and the multiple coats (more thinner) means that spraying lacquer puts a relatively large amount of

The Shimrin paints are a universal basecoat that can be clearcoated with urethane or lacquer. They dry fast and come in a wide range of colors making them ideal for graphics work.

With the right preparation and primer, urethane paints are good enough to paint nearly anything, including aluminum engine parts.

VOCs in the atmosphere. The VOC issue means that the day may come when lacquer paints are no longer available.

URETHANE

Most of the custom painting being done today is being done with urethane. Technically, urethane like our Kosmic Kolor is an enamel, yet it sprays much like a lacquer. Urethane is a two-part paint material catalyzed with an isocyanate. Even though it's classed as an enamel, urethane dries very fast and offers easy spot repairs. The fast drying means quick application of second coats, easy candy paint jobs and fast tape outs for flame jobs and graphics. Unlike lacquer, urethane is super durable, resisting rock chips and chemical stains better than almost anything. We offer urethanes that you can use as a one shot application, as a basecoat-clearcoat or as a tri-coat system.

BASECOATS

Obviously the easiest way to go with a complete paint job is with a basecoat, clearcoat. Simply put your basecoat down, get a nice even application and then let that flash for 15 or 20 minutes and come in with your clearcoats. We recommend a 75 percent overlap on the application of basecoats because they're never applied wet. You always apply a basecoat in what we call a medium coat. If you put a medium coat on with the gun too far away, you're going to stucco the job. You should be painting in the four to five, to maximum, six inch distance away from the vehicle, so that you're putting it on evenly but not wetting it. This way the proper orientation takes place, which the base coats are meant to do.

Now of course, we have developed candy-basecoats that take on the candy look and they're much easier to apply than a straight candy. But

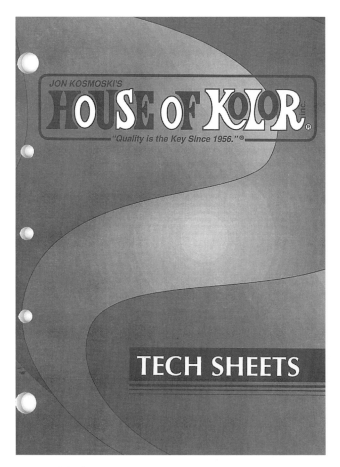

Available free from House of Kolor, the tech sheets offer detailed advice on mixing and applying all of our paint products.

then again you still have to be careful with gun adjustments, gun distance and your basic application technique. Remember not to mix systems, that is, if you're doing a lacquer job, stay with lacquer throughout, don't clearcoat the lacquer with urethane.

KUSTOM PAINTS
KANDY AND PEARLS

A kandy is really a tinted clear. A very strong pigment that holds up in small amounts and gives you that transparency through to the underbase. That's what translates to the extra depth that you see when you look into a candy paint job. It's a layering of color. Kandy layers and the clearcoats must be applied in a timely fashion, being careful to follow recommendations for flash times and overlap.

When applying our kandys and pearls you have to be careful with gun distance and the adjustments. If you're too far away blotchiness will take place. Or if you're pulling the trigger too hard you'll get blotches and those blotches will follow you throughout the whole job. It does require some expertise in gun adjustments and understanding how to hold the gun.

A pearl is like a very small metallic, but the pearl paints have a tendency to glow in the light - you get that glow as light reflected back from the pearl platelets. We have pearls available in a

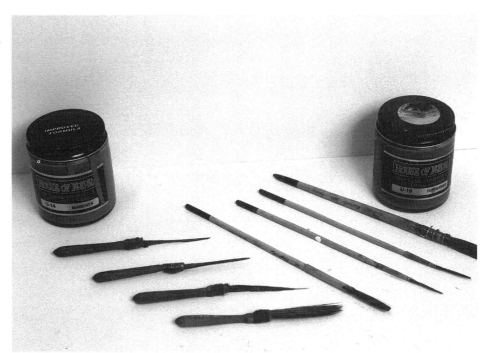

Pinstripe brushes, seen on the left, and lettering quills are both available in a variety of sizes rated numerically.

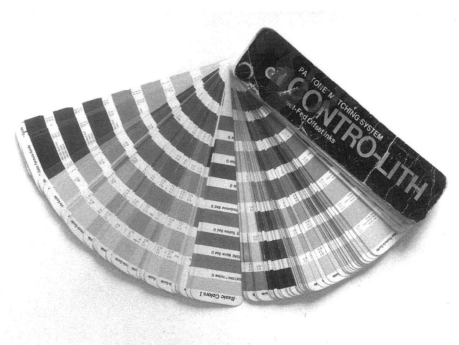

A PMS book is nothing more than a series of color swatches which provide a good means of comparing colors to see how they work together.

number of different forms: powders, paste, pre-mixed, semi-transparent and interference pearls.

Adjusting the equipment is the key to getting the pearl on evenly too. And if you're doing pearl or kandy remember that the basecoat must be applied evenly first. We have information available on gun set up, we have numerous guns and air-brushes in our shop. Because we spray with everybody's equipment we can offer help as to the best use of your own airbrush or spray gun. If you're not sure which air cap and needle to use, call our tech line for help (see the Sources at the back of the book).

The most exciting of the new products at House of Kolor are the Kameleon Kolors. These paints, made up of very specialized pigments, literally change color depending on the direction and

A custom paint job is only as good as the primer and body work underneath. Our EP-2 and KP-2 provide excellent adhesion and tremendous corrosion resistance.

type of lighting. Unlike a pearl that might have a subtle "flip-flop" effect, there's nothing subtle about the dramatic way these paints change color. If you're looking for something new. Something that no on else has, either for a great graphic effect or for the entire vehicle, check out our new Kameleon Kolors. (Note, the flames applied to the motorcycle parts in chapter 6 are done in the new Kameleon Kolors.)

CLEAR AND CLEARCOATS

Though many graphics painters and airbrush artists leave the clearcoats for someone else to apply, the following section is included in hopes it will help everyone choose, and in some cases apply, the right clear for a given situation. For more hands-on information about clearcoats see the painting sequences in Chapters Six and Seven.

At House of Kolor we now make four different clears. Certain parts of the country now are getting very sensitive to amount of volatile organic compounds in the paints. Sometimes, if you're doing motorcycle work or working in a small area you want a fast setting clear that gets very hard overnight. We think this is important if you're doing artwork and you want to get a clear that will give you a good build up and be extremely hard the next day, so that when you go to recoat you're not going to have shrinkage.

This particular clear, our UC-1, uses the same catalyst that goes into our candies, the KU-100, and it dries extremely hard the next day. The UC-1 is an excellent fuel-proof clear. It resists nitromethane fuels. It's got a solid content ready to spray of about 30 to 31 percent. As I said, it's not our highest percentage of solids clear, but it does get hard quickly. It's an excellent all around clear. It doesn't have the gloss, however, of our UFC-1 which is about a 39 or 40 percent solids clear. That's ready to spray again, once the catalyst and the reducer are mixed in, and these are all done with the 2:1:1 ratio. Two parts of clear, one part of catalyst, one part of reducer.

The reducer is the same in all of our products. The catalyst varies with different products. The UFC-1 uses the KU-500 catalyst and you cannot intermix the catalysts. The dry times will not be accurate. There are radical differences in the way

completion. We think 24 hours is the minimum time you should wait to buff those to make sure that all of the solvents have left the clearcoat. There's no point in buffing something twice, because it's still drying.

Now we've come out with another clear for the most stringent requirements in California, and that's our UFC-80. It uses the KU-800 catalyst. This clear is 80 percent solids ready to spray. It does require that you use fewer coats because

Our Kosmic reducers are made up of the finest ingredients and come in three versions. For painting smaller items in warmer environments we recommend the RU-310.

the catalysts are made. I get a kick out of painters who buy universal or aftermarket generic catalysts and try to use them in our products. They find out very quickly that this is not the way to go. The savings are not worth the problems that you can encounter trying to use outside products.

That goes with our reducer as well. Our ingredients are the best in the industry. We don't take any short cuts. We don't use filler solvents. Ours is the best that money can buy. That's what equates to long lasting paint jobs. It's not uncommon for us to hear of paint jobs 15 years old, done with our products and still looking good.

We've come out with another clear for the VOC sensitive areas, and that's our UFC-40 which is 52 percent solids ready to spray. It uses the KU-400 catalyst. It's a beautiful clear.

All of these clears buff very easily. The UC-1 is the clear that you want to buff the next day. Don't let that clear set for long periods of time, because it's very difficult to buff later because it gets so hard so quickly. The UFC-1 and the UFC-40 are excellent clears to buff, but the ideal time to buff those is within the first five to seven days of their

Metal flakes are available in raw form allowing you to mix your own metallic paint. A variety of sizes and colors are available.

27

of its high solids content. One coat of this material is nearly the same as three coats of the UC-1. The main problem we've had with the UFC-80 has been painters putting on the same number of coats as they have with other clears. It's not required. You can get all the clear that you need in two coats.

A little reducer can be used, (thankfully we have a VOC-free reducer, RU-300). depending on your location. Northern California, for example, is not as stringent as southern California and some reducer can be added. It doesn't take very much reducer to make this a very, very nice clear to work with. This is our line up of clears. Each one has its own little idiosyncrasies in how it works. All of them have excellent pot life.

There are a few guidelines for using our clears (and additional information in the tech sheets). Don't mix your candy or your clear that contains catalyst until you're ready to use it. Some people down in the hot, humid climates - Louisiana, Texas - have gone ahead and mixed large quantities of this material hours before they're ready to paint, and when they come back to do the painting they've found that their material has turned to Jello.

Don't buy large quantities or containers of catalyst if you don't intend to use them up within a week or two. Once you break the seal on the catalyst can and you pour some out you eliminate the nitrogen blanket. Once that blanket is poured out the product becomes sensitive to air in the can.

Most painters don't clean the threads of the can after they open it. Once you put a pliers on that cap you start losing your seal. Then the remaining catalyst will gain viscosity. They will get thicker and they will also pick up, unbeknownst to you, seeds that are very much like metallics. If you

It's a good idea to strain the clear through a very fine filter or a set of Kimwipes. By eliminating any small chunks in the clear you eliminate lumps in the final coat of clear.

ever put old catalyst into something and you spray it and it has an even pattern of "dirt" in it, you can look directly to your catalyst as being the culprit. Because it will pick up these clear seeds that will go through a strainer like metallic, but they'll show as dirt in the paint job.

We highly recommend buying smaller quantities of the catalyst. This is very important because most other products have very long shelf lives, the catalyst is one that does not.

On the safety side, remember that the catalyst is most dangerous when you're pouring it. You should protect yourself during pouring. Keep it off your skin. Don't breath it when it's a free monomer like this. When it mixes in the paint it becomes less hazardous, but then it's hazardous again when it's an airborne particle and you can ingest it in your respiratory system. Over long periods of painting, this can lodge in your organs and cause life-threatening things to take place.

Always wear the proper respirator. The TC19C, air-supply hood, is recommended. You don't want these materials on your skin. Wear eye protection because it can enter your body through your eyes or any mucous membrane.

SPECIALIZED PAINTS
WATER BASED PAINTS
There are some new water-based sign painting enamels designed for brush

Companies like 3M sell polishing "systems" that include two or three grades of compound or polish, and the correct polishing pads for each step of the process.

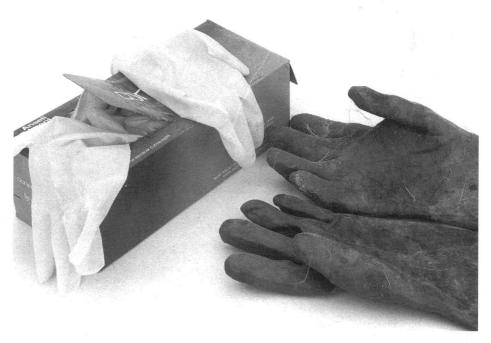

Don't get paint on your skin, even when mixing the relatively non-toxic lacquers. Always use gloves when handling and mixing paints and don't use thinners to wash your hands.

lettering and airbrush work. Designed to be used for graphics, these paints are handy because they won't react with the solvent-based paints they might be sprayed over, or the clearcoats that are often applied over the graphics.

Pinstriping and sign painting materials

The paints used for striping fall into two categories, striping enamel or striping urethane. All of these paints are designed to be inert, meaning they are meant to go on over other paints without any reaction between the two paints. The two enamels most commonly used are One Shot sign-painting enamel, and Chromatic lettering enamel. Both are enamels and both can be easily wiped off if you make a mistake.

At House of Kolor we offer the only true urethane striping paint, our Urethane Striping and Lettering Enamel, available in a wide array of super-bright colors. It can be applied as a topcoat with catalyst added, or used without a catalyst if you intend to clearcoat the stripes. This material is designed for striping, lettering and airbrush work. High pigmentation and low solids means a minimal edge and long "open time." Our Striping and Lettering Enamel may be topcoated with acrylic lacquer, urethane or acrylic enamel. When catalyzed with KU-200, our Striping and Lettering clear, UC-3, makes a good sizing for gold leaf work.

Unlike the oil-based striping enamels, which call for very long dry times before being clearcoated with urethane clear, this Striping Enamel can be clearcoated two to four hours after application.

When using our striping

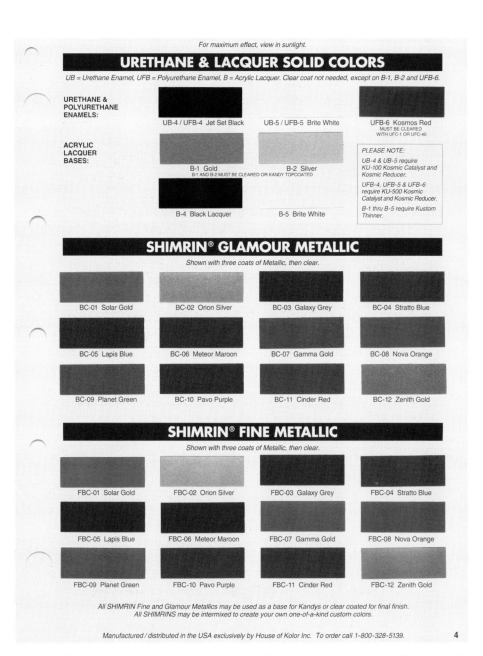

A paint chip chart can be a great creative tool allowing you to examine all the possible colors and how those colors work together.

enamel in an airbrush, reduce it 100 to 150% with RU-310 reducer. This will provide good spray-ability and fast dry times. In hot weather you may, however, want to use RU-311 instead. It's always a good idea to strain the materials though a fine mesh strainer when using them in an airbrush.

TAPE AND TAPE PRODUCTS

Tape might seem too simple to need a separate section. Yet people make the mistake of using the wrong tape, or don't understand all the tapes out there intended to make your life easier.

When you buy any masking tape, be sure to buy brand name tape meant for work on automobiles and motorcycles. 3M makes some interesting products that make these jobs easier. For taping complex patterns with sharp curves, they make plastic tape, sometimes called Fine Line tape. This material can be stretched into some pretty complex shapes without tearing like conventional masking tape. The other interesting material is called Fine Line Striping tape. This tape is like having ten rolls of narrow tape combined on one cardboard tube. You roll the tape on across the tank, then pull out one of the "pull outs." This leaves a thin stripe ready for paint with tape on either side of it. Need two lines? just apply paint to the first pull out, then pull

another and paint that one in a different color. Finesse also makes a similar product, more information on both these specialized tapes can be found in Chapter Three.

More dramatic than a pearl, the new Kameleon Kolors actually change color with the angle of the light.

Brush, Stripe and Gold Leaf Work

Old World Skills/High Tech Designs

Graphics is synonymous with airbrush work. Yet much can be done with an old-world tool, the paint brush. This chapter is intended to answer questions regarding hand lettering, pinstriping and the use of gold leaf. Unlike some other chapters, this one offers both a materials and tools section, and hands-on sequences.

THE FINE ART OF PINSTRIPING

Pinstriping is a small, though often necessary, part of any custom paint job. We tend to think of

Pinstriping a set of flames like these requires specialized paint and paintbrushes - not to mention a large measure of skill.

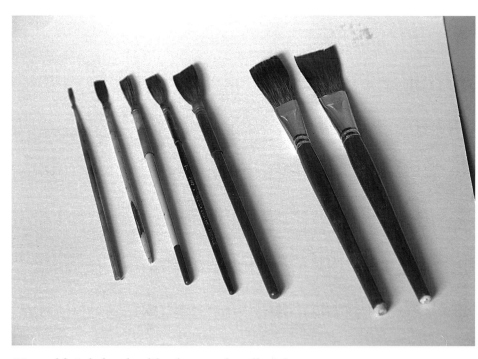

Natural bristle brushes like these work well with oil-base paint. The group on the left are quills. On the right are two flats, 5/8 and 3/4.

together.

When running "pure" pinstripes, many experienced pinstripers use two stripes of different colors. The different colors have more visual impact than a single line or two lines in one color and the two colors can work off each other as well as off the color of the vehicle to create more impact.

MATERIALS

The paints used for striping fall into two basic categories, striping enamel or striping urethane,

pinstripes as accents to a paint job or graphic layout, or sometimes just a means of cleaning up a paint edge. Yet pinstripes can be taken to the point where they actually become the design.

DESIGN IDEAS

Choosing the colors and design for the stripes on a vehicle requires experience and taste. As a color guide many pinstripers and airbrush artists use a PMS book. Designed for commercial printers, these little booklets contain hundreds of color samples and the formulas for making them. Find a color you like and hold it up next to the surface you need to stripe to see how the two colors work together. Though the book and the formulas are intended for a printer, you will get an idea how much of each basic color a particular shade contains. With help from the relatively new conversion guide, available from some art supply stores, you can even convert printer's formulas to paint mixing formulas.

Another good source of color ideas is the paint chip cards available from various paint manufacturers. Though there aren't as many hues as a PMS book, the color cards are still a good way to try various combinations to see how they work

Paint for pinstripes falls into two categories: pinstriping enamel like One-Shot or Chromatic, or Urethane Striping Enamel from House of Kolor. Pinstriping brushes come in synthetic or natural fibers, rated from number 5 to a number 0 (the smallest).

Jeremy recommends use of a simple tool like this, it's convenient in many situations for steadying your hand as you letter.

Before you begin hand lettering it's important to get the paint to the right consistency so it flows without running and without leaving any dry spots.

Lettering quills are designed with an "edge" to make it relatively easy to paint a line of a certain, consistent, size and end with a nice clean spear of paint.

(though some artists are beginning to use the new waterbased paints).

The two sign painting enamels most commonly used are One Shot and Chromatic lettering enamel. Both can be easily wiped off if you make a mistake. The problem comes when you decide to clearcoat these enamels with urethane clear. Reactions between the two dissimilar paints, and the resulting horror stories, are legion. There is a whole range of "folk-remedy" solutions to this problem. The only reliable way to avoid the problem, however, is to allow the pinstripes to completely cure - for one week or longer - before applying clear. An easier way to avoid the problem is to use urethane striping enamel.

House of Kolor offers the only true urethane striping paint, available in the usual wide array of super-bright colors. If can be catalyzed and applied as a topcoat, or used without a catalyst if you intend to clearcoat the stripes.

Pinstripes are applied with those funny looking brushes, the ones with the short handles and the long, long bristles. The best ones are made of camel or squirrel hair, though synthetics are slowly replacing the natural fibers. Striping brushes are rated by size, starting at five for a large brush and going to zero or double-zero for very fine work. Some stripers cut half the bristles out of a double-zero to get a *really* fine brush.

The keys to good pinstriping include learning how to correctly thin the paint and how to work enough paint up into the heel of the brush before starting on a line. Correctly thinning the paint means it won't leave dry spots and it won't run. Getting plenty of paint up into the heel of the brush means you can paint longer before going back to the card or Dixie cup for more paint (most pinstripers work off a card, usually some kind of coated paper, note the photo sequences).

Masking tape might seem like cheating, but many pinstripers use one piece of tape as a guide to run their finger along. Some artists use a product from 3M or Finesse (and perhaps others) that provides masking tape on both sides of at least two stripes. Just roll it on the vehicle, pull the appropriate sections, and apply the paint. Of course it isn't quite that simple. You still have to be sure the tape goes on straight and that all of it is stuck down to the vehicle so no paint migrates under the tape edge.

As with any paint or graphic application, before putting down a line be sure to clean the surface thoroughly with Prep Sol or a similar solvent that leaves no residue.

HAND LETTERING AND
LETTERING BRUSHES
Provided by Jeremy Vecoli
THE RIGHT TOOL FOR JOB

You're going to want to buy different brushes for different jobs and paints. Lettering brushes are only good for lettering. You can't go down to the drug store, or even the craft store, and buy the proper brushes that are going to work for lettering.

A "quill" is one kind of lettering brush. It gets the name because the hair is held on by a piece of plastic tubing. Traditionally, it was a piece of goose quill that was used. They're made out of squirrel hair and they're expensive because the ends of all the hairs line up to this perfect edge. Those are the actual ends of the hair, they didn't just cut it to length with a scissors. So they gather it by hand and when you smooth it out it will naturally get this chisel edge in one direction. When they make the brush they tie the hairs with a little wire tie that shows where that edge is.

With a lettering quill the hairs are really soft and when you bend the brush the ends of the hairs come to a nice, sharp edge. The hairs are a little longer so it can trail like a caster as you're lettering. The brush handling technique is the same whether you're using water-based or solvent-based paint, but you should buy the right brush for the paint you intend to use. The squirrel hair lettering quills, for example, are generally too limp to use with water-based paint.

The other type of lettering brushes are called *flats* which actually have a metal ferrule that attaches the hairs to the handle. These are set up in a flat configuration so you can cover a wider area and still have a nice chiseled edge on your brush.

You can also buy lettering brushes made with

Gold leaf comes in various configurations including variegated leaf. What bonds the leaf to the object is the "sizing" or special adhesive.

Lenni applies the sizing to an area defined by tape and then waits for it to get just sticky enough (so it will hold a fingerprint) before applying the leaf itself.

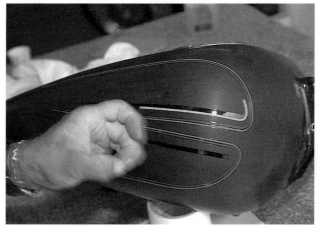

Before applying the gold leaf it's necessary first to pull the tape at the edges of the sizing.

35

The gold leaf is "applied" by pushing it up against the adhesive and then pulling away the sheet.

After the gold leaf bonds with the sizing Lenni brushes the excess leaf off with a very soft brush. In his other hand he holds a vacuum cleaner nozzle.

The final product before the clearcoats. Remember that for most designs a little gold goes a long way.

red sable, they are very expensive and automotive or solvent-based paints will ruin them. They're a little stiffer and meant to be used with Tempera paint on poster board.

CARE AND FEEDING OF YOUR BRUSHES

You have to be careful about cleaning the brushes. After you clean them you have to coat the hairs with oil. The oil keeps the little bit of paint that you couldn't get out, from drying in the heel where the bristles connect to the handle. When that paint dries and hardens it causes the hairs to fall out. After I'm done with a brush I put some Vaseline or mineral oil on the hairs. It keeps the bristles moist and I use it to form my brush and straighten the hairs before putting them away.

Brushes that are used for with water-based enamel are semi-synthetic. Those have the metal attachment, and those you clean out completely and store dry. You can't use oil-based paint on a brush that is going to be used for water-based paints because it will cause flowing problems when the oil and the water-based paint try to mix.

If you are unfamiliar with the various types of lettering brushes, get advice before committing to a purchase. A good sign supply shop can assist in your selection. Don't skimp on price. The more expensive brushes perform better and their higher cost can be spread out over a longer life span.

GOLD LEAF
WHAT IT IS

True gold leaf is made up of very, very thin sheets of 18 or 23 carat gold that can be applied to nearly any surface with a special adhesive known as sizing. The most common applications include fire trucks and the windows of banks, but that doesn't mean there is no place for gold leaf in the modern vehicle landscape.

In addition to true gold leaf, there are a variety of similar products including silver leaf (which is actually very thin sheets of aluminum), variegated gold or silver leaf, and colored materials, all of which are available from a good art supply house.

Applying gold leaf is really just a matter of cleaning the area, masking it off and applying the sizing. After allowing the sizing to set up slightly you can "stick" the leaf to the sizing, wait for that to set up further and then brush away the excess.

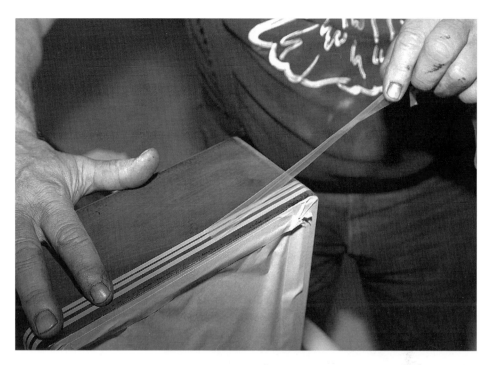

After the Finesse Striper tape is in place, it's time to pull the clear covering leaving in place the three pieces of tape that act as a stencil for the pinstripes.

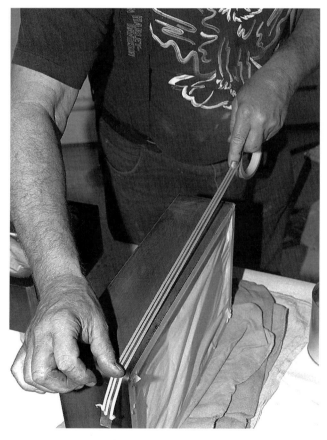

Here you can see how we ran the Finesse tape parallel to the edge of the humidor. This special tape is available in 41 different configurations.

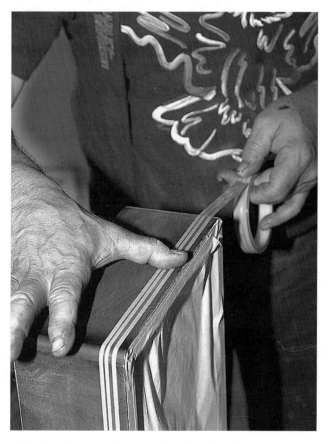

Work it down with your thumb while keeping tension on the roll.

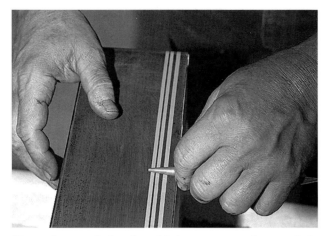

Once the tape is in place it's important to be sure it is stuck down really well. Though they make a special roller we use a brush handle.

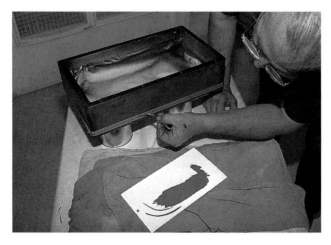

You still have to follow the basic rules of pinstriping - the paint must be correctly thinned and it's easier to pull the paint from a card or palette.

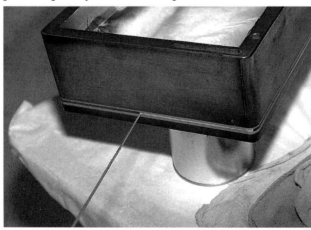

Once the painting is finished pull the tape, wait for the paint to dry and then clean up any little mistapes or areas where the paint went under the edge.

Gold leaf can be clearcoated after allowing the sizing and any pinstripes to dry, anywhere from a few hours to overnight. The extreme thinness of the sheets, on the order of only .001 inches, means that until the sizing is completely dry you can imprint or emboss a design or pattern into the gold leaf. Designs like "engine turning," or your own logo can be done with a small felt tool or a die of your own manufacture.

While these techniques might seem best suited to those very traditional applications mentioned earlier, a little leaf is a great way to add a touch of class to an elegant vehicle or design.

HAND-ON SEQUENCES
SEQUENCE NUMBER ONE

Gold leaf application with Lenni Schwartz at Krazy Kolors.

This sequence shows how to apply a piece of gold leaf to a gas tank, a task that's actually easier than it seems. Though gold leaf isn't what you'd call common, a little bit can add a certain elegance or class to a paint job or graphic. Follow along as Master Lenni adds two thin spears of gold on each side of a certain guinea-pig Harley-Davidson tank.

This gas tank has been painted and clearcoated before, which means that Lenni starts by scuffing it with wet 600 grit paper. The idea is to knock down the shine so the next layers of paint will stick, but Lenni warns the overzealous, "You have to be careful, depending on how much clear is on there, you don't want to go through that clearcoat." The next step is a thorough cleaning with a final wash.

Lenni lays out the design with 3M fine line tape, explaining as he does, "The gold leaf will be contained within the two small taped areas on either side of the tank. It's going to be a pretty strong design, we don't want to overpower the rest of the design with gold leaf."

Sizing is the "glue" that's used to bond the thin layer of gold to the gas tank and Lenni applies the sizing with a small brush straight out of the bottle. As a rule of thumb, the sizing should be allowed to set-up until you can push your finger against it and leave a fingerprint. Lenni puts some on an inconspicuous spot and tests it there before applying the gold leaf.

When the sizing is the right stickiness and the tape is removed, Lenni pushes the gold leaf (with the backing) up against the adhesive and pulls it away, which leaves a strip of gold leaf attached to the sizing. He continues along the spear in this fashion until he has the entire area covered with gold leaf.

Lenni allows the sizing to dry for at least 30 minutes before brushing the excess gold leaf off *very* gently so as not to scratch the gold. The brush he uses is actually his wife's makeup brush, though any very soft-bristle brush would work.

Once the excess gold leaf is brushed off the only thing left is the pinstriping. The pinstripes clean up the edge of the gold and adds to the design with the color. Lenni lays down the teal stripes with Urethane Lettering Enamel from House of Kolor and a pinstriping brush.

Once the pinstripes are finished the only thing left is the clearcoat - a job for Mallard Teal in St. Paul, Minnesota. Because the striping paint is a urethane this tank can be clearcoated without any worries about a reaction between the urethane clear and the striping paint. Lenni adds that though you can clear the gold leaf right away, he prefers to wait a few hours or overnight if possible. **Sequence number two:** Jon Kosmoski pinstripes a set of cigar boxes.

This short sequence shows the use of a tool that's very handy when it comes time to do simple pinstriping.

Actually, these aren't "cigar boxes," they're humidors sent to me to be painted and pinstriped. After painting them we decided to run a pinstripe along the top and bottom of the boxes. For the bottom of the humidors I though it would be easier to use the Finesse tape.

What I like about this product is the fact that you can buy it in any configuration, any combination of stripes, single, double or whatever, with nearly any spacing you want. If there's a trick to using this tape, the trick is to make sure it is stuck down. Before applying the tape I buzzed the surface of the humidors with P600, a 3M paper applied to a flat-sanding DA, then wiped the surface down carefully with a final wash.

Once the tape is positioned I go over it again

Here we see Craig Smith as he applies the decal lettering to the saddle bag and peels back the transfer paper.

The next step is to outline the letters with black paint applied with a lettering quill.

To make a pattern of the exact logo, Craig tapes tracing paper over a decal so he can "pounce" the paper and thus make a pattern.

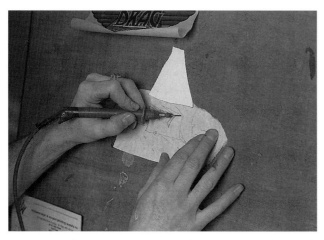

Some people use a pounce wheel, Craig use the electro-pounce which punches tiny holes in the tracing paper.

With the pattern taped over the lettering on the bag and a towel full of baby powder Craig pounces the paper, which will leave tell-tale pattern of dust.

Using the lines of dust as his guide, Craig paints in the horizontal lines and the lines on the top of the logo.

to make sure it's stuck down. They make a little roller that you can use to go over the tape to ensure it's stuck down and it's probably a good tool to use. The tape is applied to three coats of cobalt KBC-5 sprayed over a black base, BC-25. I use the Finesse tape on the bottom of the humidors but the top of these fancy boxes will be done free hand.

Just like free-hand pinstriping you have to be sure the paint has the right consistency and to do that it's best to work off a palette, without the palette you can't feel how thick the paint is. The paint will start to heavy-up as you work, when it does I add U-00 striping reducer to our Striping and Letting enamel to make it flow.

It's easier to pull the tape early so the paint doesn't try to climb the tape edge and make a big ledge. In places where the paint creeps under the edge of the tape you can go in later and peel it off with the X-Acto knife.

The trick to pinstriping, with or without the tape, is to thin the paint correctly and to load the paint up into the brush. I always twist the brush as I pull it through a turn, it's the only good way to get a consistent line (in terms of thickness) through the corner.

There's only one other key to good pinstriping: practice, practice, practice.

SEQUENCE NUMBER THREE: Craig Smith pinstripes a set of flames.

This sequence actually finishes the Harley-Davidson parts that we painted for the Drag Specialties bike (see Chapter Six). The pinstriping is done by Craig Smith, well known Minneapolis pinstripe artist. In addition to standard pinstriping, Craig shows us how he creates the true look of a Drag Specialties logo with the outline already painted on the bags and the letters from an actual decal.

To start the job Craig cuts out two blocks of letters from a Drag Specialties decal, then sticks a piece of pre-mask or transfer paper of the top of each one. Now he cuts out the actual letters from the decal, peels the adhesive from the back and sticks the whole piece to the bag between the tape lines already positioned there. With the letters positioned on the bag Craig removes the transfer paper and guide tape, and outlines the letters with black urethane Striping and Lettering enamel.

Craig likes to use the paint as it comes out of the can, though he admits not everyone agrees. "Some people like to thin the paint, but I find it goes on nice just as it comes out of the can. If I thin it then the line might get too wide." The brush Craig uses is a squirrel hair lettering brush, probably a number one or a zero. Though he tends to use the paint as it comes out of the can, he does put it on a palette and draws the paint from the palette.

Once the letters and outline are done, Craig lays tracing paper over an uncut decal and marks the position of the black lines on the original. An electro pounce is used to make the series of tiny holes that mark the lines on the tracing paper. Then he tapes the pounced paper onto the bag, "pounces" the paper - with baby powder if it's a dark background or charcoal if it's a light background. Now he can use more Urethane Striping & Lettering enamel to paint the horizontal lines in exactly the same place they are on the decal.

Once the lines are finished Craig paints the silver outline with a similar brush. Again, Craig takes paint straight from the can, puts some on a card or palette and then takes the paint from the card.

Once the logo is outlined Craig moves on to the outlines of the flames on the saddle bags and the other parts. Craig often uses one hand to steady the other, in this way he creates nice even pinstripes. As he says, "The key to a straight lines is to have paint of the right consistency and use the right brush. If I get enough paint worked up into the brush I can go almost all the way down the side of a Cadillac without having to load up the brush again."

Note, there are a variety of ways and more than a little controversy over the best way to store the long pinstriping brushes, Craig Smith uses the following recipe: "I leave mine in mineral spirits mixed fifty-fifty with straight 50 weight oil. Some guys leave them in ATF, or Dexron to be more precise, then run them through the mineral spirits before using them again."

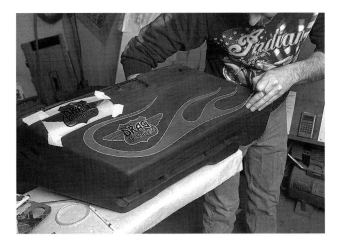

Once the logo is outlined Craig can proceed to outline the flames with a silver, urethane striping paint.

This is a good example of the way Craig "rolls" the striping brush as he moves through a tight curve on the inside of a flame.

Note the way the brush has rolled and also how Craig supports and steadies the brushing hand with the other.

Before she starts the pinstriping Nancy scuffs the fender (everything has been clearcoated) with wet 400 or 500 grit paper.

Sequence number four:
Nancy Brooks pinstripes a fender.

In this set of photos Nancy Brooks from Brooks Signs pinstripes the fender from the Dave Perewitz bike seen in Chapter Six.

The paint used in this project is the Urethane Striping & Lettering Enamel. As mentioned earlier, this paint can be used either catalyzed or non-catalyzed. Because this paint will be clearcoated Nancy uses the paint in non- catalyzed form.

Choosing the right colors for the pinstripes is nearly as important as the stripes themselves. "Sometimes I use a complimentary color," explains Nancy. "Unless I don't want the area to stand out, then I use a color that's close to the color of the overall graphic design. I will often add a color that throws everything off, to 'give it an edge.' Something you'd never expect like a lime green on

a purple job." Nancy mixes colors for striping in order to get enough variety. "I like to see new colors, if you don't mix colors you're limited as to what's available."

For the brushes Nancy commonly uses Langnickel sign painting brushes and Mack stripers though she is beginning to use Langnickel Russian squirrel hair brushes. "They're expensive," admits Nancy, "but as they break down they're still usable, just smaller. For areas with jagged lines I like a short sign painting brush, for that situation they're better than the long striping brush."

Like most pinstripers Nancy takes the paint from a palette. "Working off the palette aligns the bristles of the brush and helps me to feel the consistency of the paint. As the paint dries on the card I add reducer to give it the right consistency."

Nancy starts the pinstriping by taking purple off the card and applying it to one of the rips that runs along the length of the fender.

Here you can see how the purple was applied to the rips that run along both sides of the fender. The purple is a mix, Nancy seldom uses paint right out of the can.

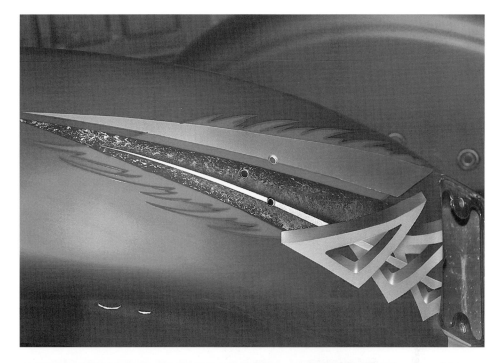

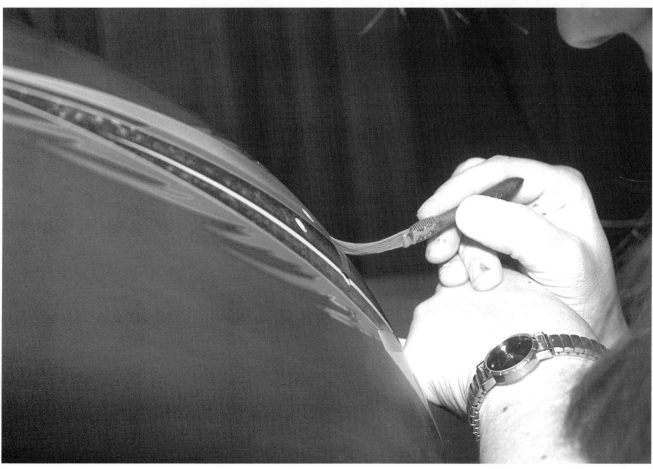

For the relatively long pinstripes Nancy uses a striping brush, but for short sections or jagged lines she often uses a lettering brush. Note again how one hand supports the other.

Chapter Four

Design and Tapeouts

You need more than just paint

Before starting a complex layout on a car, truck or bike (or boat for that matter) you first need a good design. Once you've drawn out the design and received approval from the customer you need the ability to mask it off or tape it out.

Obviously, when the masking is done you need the ability to apply the paint in an efficient and safe fashion.

This chapter deals briefly with the first part of the dilemma, creating a good design. We offer

What started as a sketch became a colorful graphic. With just a little help from some computer cut vinyl *and a couple of talented artists.*

insights from other artists and ideas for improvement. The rest of the chapter contains painting sequences, with the emphasis on the layout and masking, rather than on the painting itself.

The methods used range from "conventional" masking with fine line and masking tape, to the use of computer-cut masks. As always, one method isn't right and the other wrong. They all work, it's up to you to decide which methods fits your type of work, experience and equipment.

THE ART OF DESIGN

A good design is a nebulous thing, something you know when you see it. Yet "it" remains an intangible, easier to identify than to quantify. In the realm of Graphics, good design includes not only the shape but the colors as well.

If you ask one of the masters like Nancy Brooks where she gets her ideas, she replies that they come from other artists' designs, but also from nearly everything she sees. She sites the skateboard magazines as having some of the wildest, newest designs, but readily admits that her ideas come from other sources as well. Dave Perewitz, who builds the bikes Nancy puts many of her design on, reports that his owns idea come from "almost anything, including Street Rod magazines and the interior design of new houses."

Andy Anderson says that,

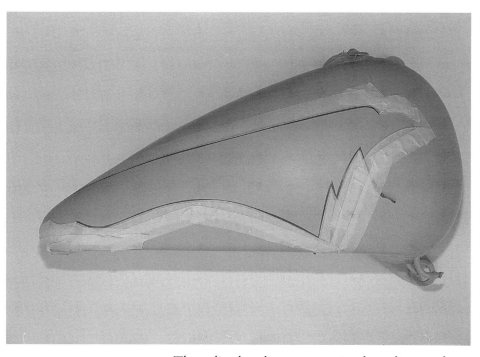

The stylized eagle starts as a simple outline on the gas tank, done to match the sketch by Ken Madden. Bruce uses 3M plastic tape to do the outline.

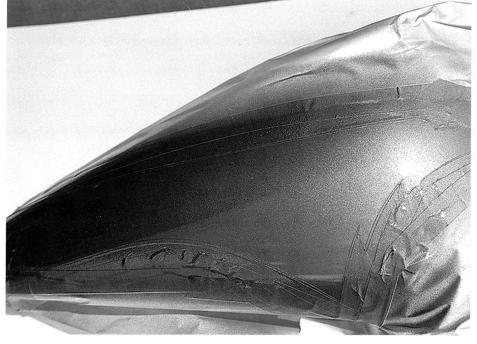

After applying black to the back, and orion silver to the front of the "bird," Bruce has the beginnings of his design.

After applying a clearcoat and scuffing that surface, Bruce puts down the fine line tape that will help define the wings.

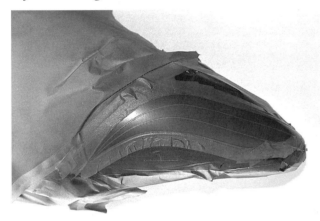

This is one of the tanks after application of the basecoat and Kandy burgundy. Typically, each color application is clearcoated, and that is the next step

When the tape across the wings is pulled, the taped areas become pinstripes across the wings - they even show the underlying fade from black to silver.

"Many of my ideas come from the great custom painters of the 1960s, men like Art Himsl. And I've always been impressed with the work of Nancy Brooks and Ray Mason. I try to pick up the 'annuals' produced for the Art, Illustration or Design fields. There's a wealth of creative-ness in them. The trick is to open up, take it all in and let your creativity do the rest."

If you spend time with Leah Begin, you find that though she has no formal training in art or in airbrushing, her work is very high in quality. When you see all the books from other airbrush artists in her small office you realize that she spends a lot of time studying the work of other artists. As Leah explains, "You have to be looking all the time for new ideas."

Artists doing Graphics need to remember that good Graphics involves two very separate abilities: design and application. In other words, you need to be both a technician, able to apply paint and understand all the materials; and you need to be an artist, able to do designs and layouts that compliment the vehicle and please the customer.

In assessing your own abilities you must be brutally honest. If in his critique you find one area missing, you must work at improving those abilities that are lacking. The technical abilities are easier to improve as many Vo-tech schools offer airbrushing and sign painting classes. And magazines like AutoGraphics and Airbrush Magazine list both how-to articles and information on seminars staffed by well-known artists.

SEQUENCE NUMBER ONE:

Graphic eagles at Wizard Custom Studios.

This sequence is done by Bruce Bush at Wizard Custom Studios in Ham Lake, Minnesota, just north or Minneapolis. Instead of cutting out a mask ahead of time, either with a computer or by hand, Bruce simply does his layouts with tape and the painting with a full size paint gun. Of note is the way Bruce applies his pinstripes, without the aid of a pinstripe brush.

Bruce starts the project by outlining the eagle design with plastic tape, both 1/16 and 1/8 inch, from 3M. Once he has an outline that looks like the sketch done earlier by artist Ken Madden, Bruce masks around the outside of the thin tape

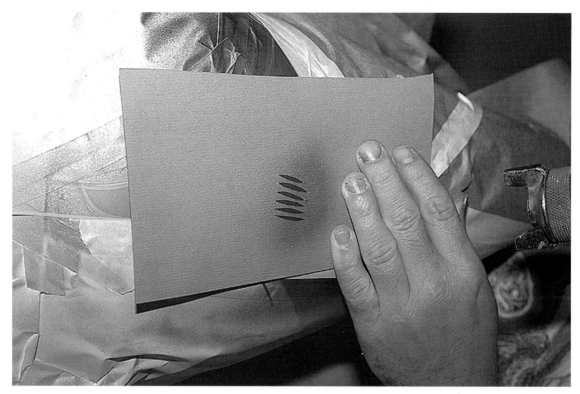

The stencil Bruce uses to do the "feathers" is a very simple affair made from a piece of light board. Instead of making one stencil big enough to do the entire area Bruce simply moves this small stencil across the bird in a random fashion.

Protected by clearcoats the finished bird exhibits glow-in-the-dark eyes, a nice feathered pattern and pinstripes that didn't have to be done at the end of the job.

We come into this job at Let's Get Graphic as Lenni applies transfer paper to the vinyl that's already been cut on the plotter/cutter.

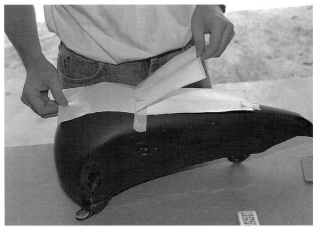

The vinyl for one tank, with the wax paper backing and the transfer paper on top, is taped in place across the middle with a piece of masking tape.

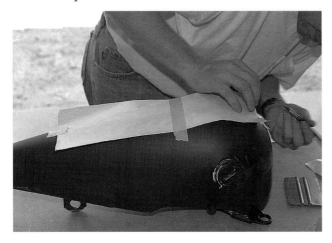

Half the vinyl is pulled back, then the wax backing paper is removed and that half is stuck down onto the tank.

with 3/4 inch masking tape and then uses masking paper for the rest of the tank. Bruce likes to create the pinstripe first, instead of going back in and doing a conventional pinstripe later.

To create the pinstripe in this fashion the outline color is sprayed first, then 1/8th inch tape is laid in right at the inner edge of the outline. The paint under this 1/8th inch tape is the pinstripe. After laying down the 1/8th inch tape it is necessary to cover the seam between the pinstripe tape the layout tape with 3/4 inch masking tape. Then the rest of the tapeout can proceed (note, after laying down the tape a light coat of SG-100 can be sprayed to "seal" the tape line and prevent bleed-unders).

This design incorporates a fade from silver to black and Bruce starts the painting by applying black basecoat, PBC-43 black pearl, to the back of the bird. Bruce explains that with a fade, "The closer the two colors are the easier it is to make a nice fade. In this case I paint the black first because the silver is next, the metallic color should always be the second color." The black is applied in two light coats, with about a ten minute flash time between coats, done with a conventional siphon-style spray gun.

Bruce does the blend from silver to black in two steps: First he paints the front of the eagle with BC-02 orion silver where there is no black, but that leaves little transition between the black and the silver. Next he dilutes the silver with additional clear, SG-100, adds more reducer for the clear, and then a little extra reducer for adhesion (it is being sprayed pretty dry). This second coat is sprayed mostly in the area between the silver and the black, during this second application of silver Bruce "fans" the gun, turning it with his wrist so the mist is lighter in one direction.

Bruce puts a different cap on the spray gun, one better suited to spraying a clearcoat, and applies two medium coats of UC-1 clear. This is done because you can't sand on pearl or metallics. When the clearcoat is dry Bruce scuffs it with a grey Scotch Brite pad.

At this point Bruce lays the 1/8th inch tape around the inside of the masked area so the "pin-

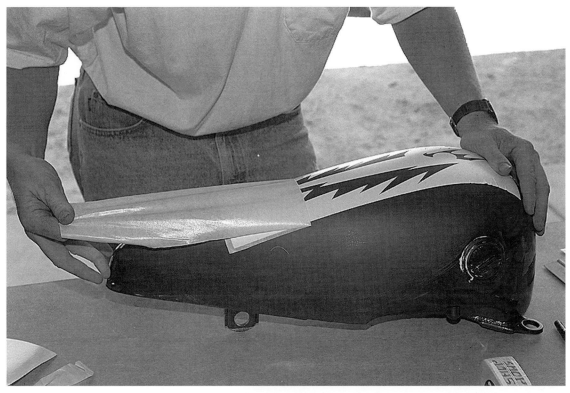

After the entire piece of vinyl has adhered to the tank, the transfer paper is removed from the top. As mentioned in the text, part of this design was pulled out before the transfer paper was put in place.

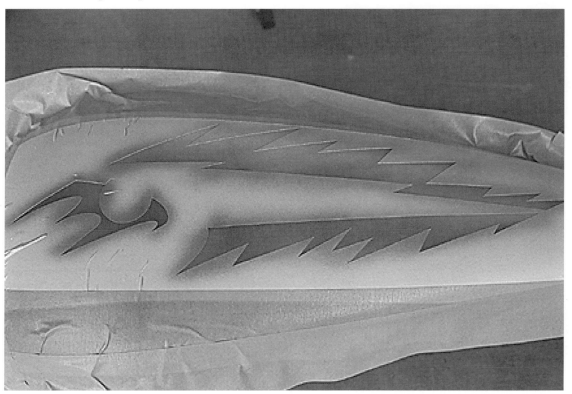

With the outer parts of the design removed, that area is sprayed with silver basecoat.

stripe" fades from silver to black. After laying out the pinstripe tape and some 3/4 inch tape to cover the seam, Bruce can begin laying out the rest of the design.

First the area must be cleaned with a tack rag, then the design for the wings is laid out freehand with fine line tape, finally the rest of the tanks is masked off. As he is working Bruce tries to keep his hands off the surface to be painted so no oils are transferred from his hands to the

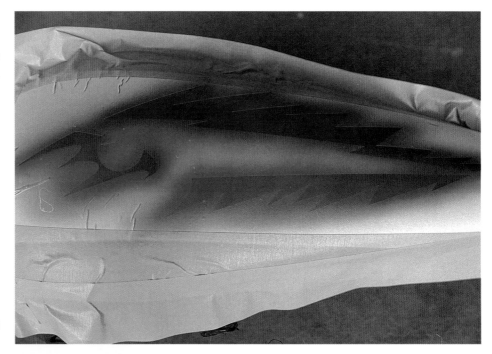

Once the silver basecoat has flashed the next step is a coat of light teal.

surface. It's a good idea to keep the design or sketch near by for reference. Also, Bruce always does the two tank halves at the same time so he can keep everything even and symmetrical.

After the taping is done Bruce puts down two coats of BC-11 cinder red as a base, followed by two medium coats of the UK-6 kandy burgundy. He waits for each coat to flash before applying the next. As a test he touches a non-critical area with his finger, when touched the paint surface should be sticky but not "string up" as he pulls his finger away.

Bruce uses RU-310 reducer here with both the BC and the UK series paints, because it's a hot day and he wants to get in and cover the parts quickly. After waiting for the kandy to flash the first of two coats of the UC-1 urethane clearcoat are applied.

Now the tape is pulled. Note, the thin tape lines that were run across the wings are now pinstripes that show the underlying fade and also define the wings. Bruce likes to pull the tape earlier rather than later. This way the clear is still flowing when the tape is pulled and the tape edge will soften. It's also less likely that the tape will pick up the paint as it is pulled away from the surface. The

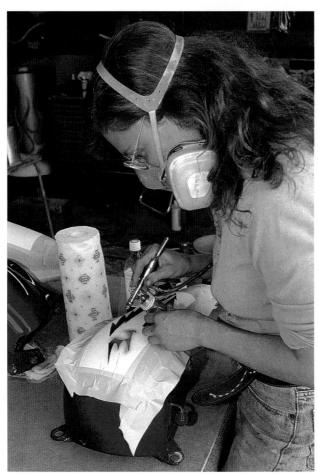

Leah runs the airbrush off shop air at nearly 60 psi. These airbrushes are designed to accept a jar, so paint can be pre-mixed into extra jars ahead of time.

down side of pulling the tape early is the fact that any debris that falls in the clear will mark it because it is wet.

Bruce lays out the beak next and sprays it in two stages, first with two coats of UK-2 kandy lime gold, and later with two coats of UK-8 kandy tangerine to give it a warmer color.

To do the bird's eyebrow Bruce simply tapes it off and applies two coats of BC-26 basecoat white. The white is then covered with two coats of UC-1 clear and allowed to dry overnight.

Now come the feathers, probably the most interesting part of this project. After masking off the area Bruce cuts a "feather stencil" from light board. "You need to use low enough pressure, about 20 psi, so you don't blow paint under the stencil," explains Bruce. "I move the stencil around randomly as I spray so it doesn't look like I used a pre-cut pattern. Some randomness makes it more realistic, if you look at a bird their feathers aren't perfect either. In fact I actually cut two different feather stencils, they're not quite the same and it helps to achieve that same effect." The feathers are sprayed in a beige color, a special paint mix created by using browns and silvers from the PBC system.

The eyes are next. After taping Bruce lays down a base of cinder red, topcoated with KG-7 glo red. This glow-in-the dark paint from House of Kolor gathers light during the day (or from a light source) and gives it off as a glow after dark, which should make for a very interesting bird especially just after the sun goes down. Though it gathers more light if applied over a white base, Bruce used a red base to give the eyes a darker red color when seen during the day. The glo material is applied in three coats with flash times between each application.

The eyes are the last step and now the tanks and the rest of the sheet metal gets clearcoated with four coats of UC-1 clear. After those topcoats have dried overnight Bruce sands lightly with wet 600 grit paper on a flexible sanding pad and then applies four more coats of clear. After color sanding and buffing that final clearcoat the surface is perfectly smooth.

The stencil is cut with a small, heated cutter. The holes have a certain randomness. Leah will test the stencil before using it on the actual job.

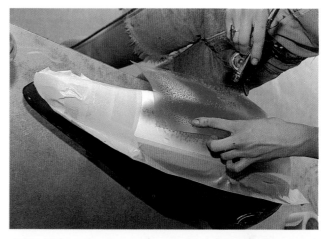

Hot pink is the next color, applied through the stencil over the teal, the idea is to create a textured pattern.

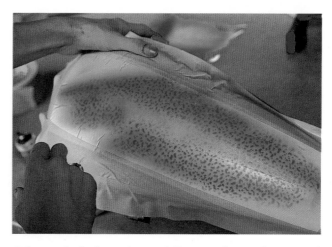

This is the light teal area following the application of the hot pink sprayed through Leah's unique stencil.

The dark shadows look out of place and won't make sense until the masking vinyl is pulled and they become part of the total design.

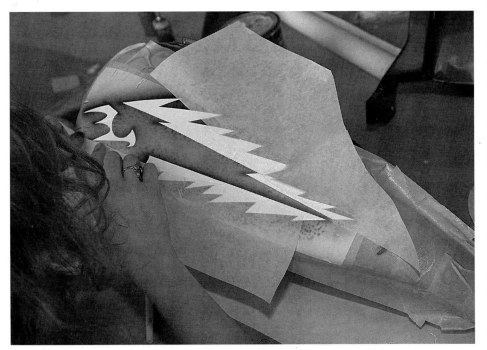

After spraying a single coat of SG-100 clear and allowing it to dry, the outer parts of the design are put back into the vinyl.

Use of computer-cut mask at Let's get Graphic.

This first sequence documents the use of a computer-cut mask at the Let's Get Graphic shop in Spring Lake Park, Minnesota. Though some people see the computer solely as a means of generating vinyl graphics the computer and cutter can also be used as a tool to cut the stencils for a design, which is then done with airbrush the same as it would be in any situation. The computer simply eliminates cutting the mask by hand or laying the whole thing out with tape, and then having to duplicate the design on the other side of the vehicle and possibly the fenders.

In this case the original design is Leah's. Lenni Hubbard, the computer guru at Let's Get Graphic, scanned the image into the computer and then used the plotter/cutter to cut out the design on Gerbermask vinyl material.

The mask itself is made up of many individual pieces, which can either be pulled off the backing and put on the tank or fenders one piece at a time, or put on in one "whole." Leah prefers to put the whole thing on, so as to avoid any trouble getting the pieces to fit later (Note, on one tank they did pull out part of the design before the mask was stuck down). "I think it's better to put the piece down complete," explains Leah. " Because the mask stretches some when it's applied and

Here the "eye" has already been painted and masked and the arch has just been painted with orange pearl.

sticks down that half of the mask.

Using a squeegee Lenni works to eliminate air bubbles in the half of the mask he just stuck down. Then he folds back the other half, peels off the wax paper and repeats the process for the second half of the design. Lenni explains that, "it helps to mark a centerline or reference point on the design to be used as an aid in correctly positioning the mask on the fender or tank." Once both halves of this way the individual pieces all stretch together."

After the masks are cut on Gerbermask (a vinyl material with a wax-paper backing), another step is required to stick the masks down on the gas tanks. Lenni and Leah cut a large piece of pre-mask (sometimes called transfer paper), which is sticky on the back side, and stick this over the Gerbermask. Leah explains that not everyone uses this additional layer of paper but, "There's no other way to hold that mask together and accurately position it, especially on a rounded object. The pre-mask holds everything in place so all the shapes that make up the design remain consistent." Lenni adds the fact that the adhesive used on the pre-mask paper is a wax base and stays with the paper so it doesn't react with the paint or inhibit the paint's adhesion later.

The pre-mask is set over the entire piece of Gerbermask. Now Lenni positions this three-layer sandwich (transfer paper, vinyl and wax paper backing) on the tank and holds it in place with a piece of masking tape across the center (check the photos to relieve confusion). Next he folds back one half of the sandwich and peels off the wax paper on the back side of the Gerbermask, then

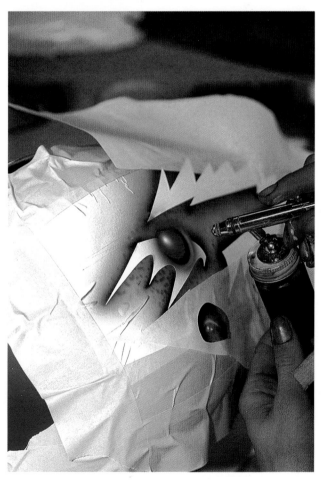

At this point the sphere (or eye) is unmasked, painted with blue with a white highlight, and will then be cleared and masked again.

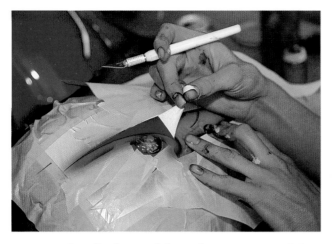

Here Leah pulls the vinyl from the center part of the design.

Then comes an application of silver that will act as a basecoat for the colors that follow. Note the white highlight running through the center of this section.

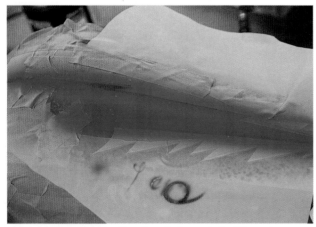

The final color application is hot pink. Note the way Leah managed to create the highlight running through the center of this section. After she pulls the tape it will look just like the photo on page 44.

the mask are firmly positioned on the tank the top layer, or pre-mask, can be peeled off leaving only the vinyl.

Before starting into the airbrushing Leah makes a stencil that will be used to create a pattern in the background of the design. The stencil is made with the stencil burner, think of it as a small soldering iron, and a piece of clear acetate. Though pre-cut stencils are available Leah likes to make her own unique designs. In this case she wants the stencil big enough to cover the areas being sprayed without having to stop and re-position the stencil.

For this sequence Leah runs her airbrush at 55 to 80 psi. Before starting on the actual sheet metal Leah tries a variety of test patterns using the stencil she cut, with both light and dark colors, to examine various levels of contrast. Because airbrush orifices are smaller than those of standard spray guns Leah is careful to strain the paint into each of the small airbrush containers before she begins painting the design.

The actual painting starts with a universal silver basecoat with medium size metallic flakes. This will act as a base under the next coats. Though they could have used white, Leah prefers silver for the base because it seems to cover more quickly. Note, part of this design was pulled out of the Gerbermask paper earlier before the mask was placed on the tank.

The BC-02 orion silver is applied in one coat with the airbrush running on almost 60 psi. The next coat, PBC-57 light teal, can be applied right away because the PBCs dry quickly. In fact, the next coat can be put down as soon as the paint is flat and not wet looking. The next color, PBC-39 hot pink, is sprayed through the stencil and shows up nicely against the teal background. Before spraying a coat of SG-100 intercoat clear Leah adds dark shadows to the top and bottom of the design.

After applying the intercoat clear and allowing it to dry for nearly 30 minutes Leah replaces the pieces of the mask that were removed (it's always a good idea to save the cutout pieces). Now she pulls the round part of the design near the front, the "eye," and paints that in dark blue, with black at the edges and a white highlight. Then she puts the sphere mask back on and pulls the small arch in front of the sphere, which will be painted orange over a white base.

Next Leah pulls the center part of the mask and replaces the small orange arches just in front and behind the sphere. She applies the silver basecoat to the center area before spraying some white through the center of this section. The white will show through the topcoat and provide a highlight on the finished center "rip," thus creating a curved effect. Multiple passes of hot pink on top of the white and silver provide Leah with the deep color she is looking for. By keeping the application of hot pink somewhat lighter in the center of the design, the highlight mentioned earlier is reinforced. Now it's time to pull the tape, fix a few inevitable errors, and then clearcoat the tanks and fenders.

SEQUENCE NUMBER THREE:

Use of a pre-cut mask by Lenni Schwartz of Krazy Kolors

The idea here is to show how Lenni Schwartz from Krazy Kolors in St. Paul Minnesota works from a mask created ahead of time, instead of taping everything out with masking tape in the more conventional fashion.

Lenni starts with a sketch of the raw design, which is then transferred to a piece of Gerbermask paper. To transfer the design Lenni puts the Gerber paper on the drawing board, then lays graphite paper on top of the Gerber paper. The graphite paper is treated on the back side with a material that leaves a line behind after it is written over, like old-fashioned carbon paper. Now he lays the sketch or finished art work over the graphite paper and draws out the design, which essentially traces the design onto the Gerber paper. Lenni uses an ink pen so he can tell where he's been on the design.

With a sharp knife Lenni cuts around the outside of design so he has something to mask to. Next, he uses transfer tape, (called pre-mask paper in the previous sequence) to transfer the cut-out design to the fender, position it and stick down.

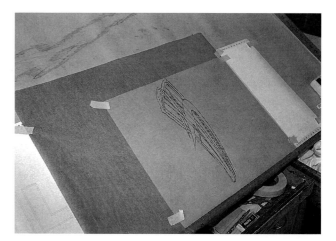

Lenni starts the job by positioning the sketch on top of a piece of graphite paper, which is positioned on the Gerbermask.

Here you can see the Gerbermask on the bottom, with the graphite paper (there are other similar papers at the art supply store that could be used here as well) and the sketch pulled back.

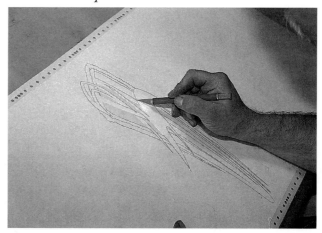

After the design is traced onto the Gerbermask Lenni cuts out most of the design with a X-Acto knife. The idea is to do the cutting here on the drawing board.

Next, transfer paper is placed on top of the vinyl, the wax backing is removed and the vinyl is placed on the fender. Here you see Lenni pulling the transfer paper.

Lenni slits any voids or air bubbles he can't eliminate and flattens them, then uses more transfer paper to mask off the rest of the rear fender.

The basecoat for this design is BC-26 white applied with an Iwata airbrush, running on about 30 psi. According to Lenni, "the white base under everything means the colors will cover faster and be much brighter."

Sunrise pearl, PBC-30, is the first color to be applied. All the pearls are mixed with RU-310 fast dry reducer, so it dries fast and can be back-taped faster. "Sometimes you have to thin it a little extra," explains Lenni, "to get it to flow good with the airbrush." Lenni mixes each color in a small Dixie cup, rather than using separate small jars, and then uses the top of an airbrush jar to reach down into each cup and feed paint to the airbrush.

Next up on the color palette is PBC-38 lime time pearl (the orange underneath is PBC-32 Tangelo). Then it's time to back-tape most of the areas that were already painted. For this Lenni uses conventional masking tape and Fine Line tape for small detail areas, adding, "The Fine Line is nice because you can see through it, so you can tell exactly where the edge should be."

After back-taping Lenni does another basecoat of white, BC 26.

On top of the white base he applies teal Striping and Lettering enamel U-16. To darken the teal and give it a different shade Lenni mixes U-9 blue with U-12 silver and sprays it onto the front of the teal area.

Now he pulls the back tape and then another arc from the original mask - exposing more orange underneath - and tapes over the recently painted

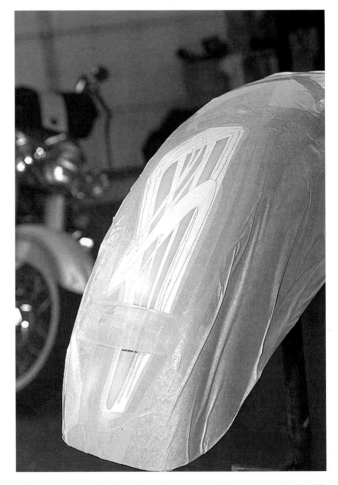

Here we see the fender after everything is masked off and a basecoat of white has been applied.

teal area. The next color to be applied is PBC-39 hot pink.

It's time for the final color, but first Lenni masks over the hot pink and uncovers the parts he wants in deep purple PBC-40. After the purple the only thing left is to pull the tape and apply the clearcoats.

SEQUENCE NUMBER FOUR:

Nancy Brooks from Brooks Signs does the layout on a Chevelle.

This incomplete sequence is more about layout and design than the actual application. The project is a Chevelle receiving graphics at the shop of Nancy Brooks and though we couldn't stay around long enough to see the finished car, there is enough information here for a good lesson in how to do a graphics layout on a larger vehicle like a car or truck.

Nancy starts off with a good photo of the

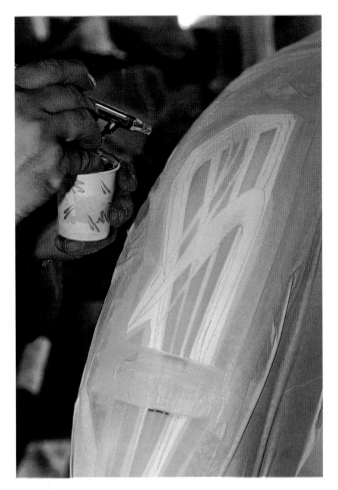

Sunrise pearl is mixed in a small Dixie cup, the Iwata airbrush draws straight from the cup.

Here we see the lime green is already applied and Lenni is pulling another piece of vinyl before spraying a new area.

vehicle. In this case a side view of the car taken from far enough back to minimize any distortion of the dimensions. With photo in hand Nancy next makes multiple copies on the Xerox machine. A series of sketches are done on these copies. The sketches evolve until Nancy has a really good graphic design. By working on a copy of a photograph she is sure the graphics will actually fit the dimensions and proportions of the car.

"Because it's a nice clean side view, I'm sure everything is in proportion. I take measurements off the sketch and then apply those to the full size drawing." Nancy goes on to explain, "Sometimes I have to make a subtle change once I have the full size paper up against the car, maybe I have to move something just a little bit because it's too close to a body line for example."

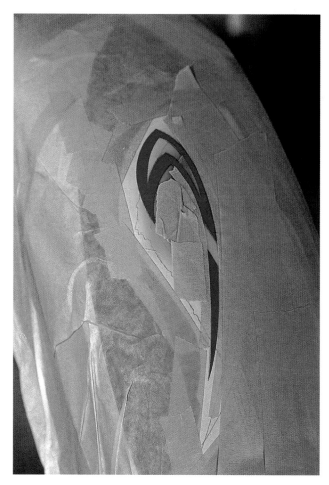

Two arcs in the center of the design have been unmasked prior to being painted. Everything else is masked off (or back taped).

Before drawing the design out full size, Nancy hangs a full size piece of paper on the car and then runs a piece of graphite over the paper so that all the body lines, creases and door handles show through.

Next she draws the art work or graphic design out full size on that same piece of paper. Then the paper is put on the light table and Nancy puts Transmask over that (on top of it). Now she can start cutting the vinyl on the light table, tracing the lines that show through from the design- being careful not to cut through to the backing sheet. Nancy adds, "sometimes in big areas I actually use regular fine line tape for the long lines. Of course the fine line tape gets put on the car before the Transmask goes on."

After the cutting is done, but before the Transmask is stuck down to the car, the pre-mask,

or transfer paper, is added on top. As Nancy explains, "This transfer paper is just used to hold everything together until the vinyl is stuck down." Because the transfer paper is transparent Nancy can see the design and reference marks through the paper.

So like the other sequences in this chapter the material placed on the car is a three-layer sandwich: A two-layer Transmask vinyl material with wax paper backing, covered with one layer of pre-mask paper.

Before any actual painting begins Nancy and crew carefully scuff the car down with 500 grit paper and plenty of water. Now it's time to place the sandwich of vinyl on the car. Nancy and crew run a piece of wide masking tape across the center of the paper to hold it to the car. Working with a helper, Nancy folds back the top half of the vinyl

Following application of a white basecoat, Lenni applies a special mix of Lettering Enamel.

sandwich, removes the wax paper backing and then sticks the vinyl on the car. A squeegee is used to eliminate air bubbles from the top half before the whole process is repeated for the lower half of the car. Once the entire sheet is securely stuck to the car, the top layer, or carrier paper can be removed.

Now Nancy has a Chevelle in the shop with the mask in place, ready to begin the airbrushing.

INTERVIEW: NANCY BROOKS,
BROOKS SIGNS

Nancy Brooks is perhaps best known as the artist who does the incredible graphics for David Perewitz's prize-winning custom Harley-Davidsons. In addition to her work for David, Nancy does sign work, as well as race cars, boats and exotic promotional vehicles for the entertainment industry.

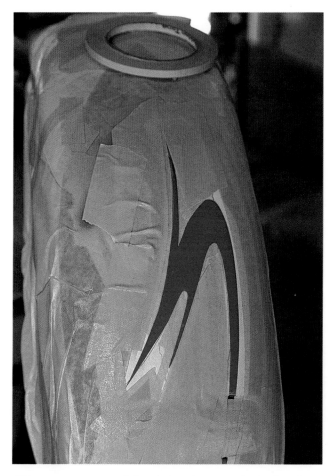

Here a new part of the design is unmasked, showing the orange color underneath.

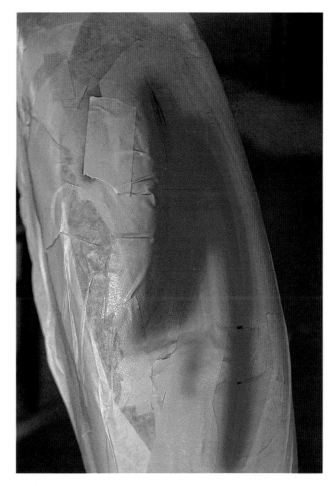

After pulling the vinyl the area is basecoated in white, then painted with hot pink.

Nancy, how did you get started in the business?

After completing my formal education (four year school of the Museum of Fine Arts, and two years Butera School of Art) I was given my first opportunity by Roy Mason at Mason Signs in Brockton, Massachusetts. Roy introduced me to custom motorcycle painting and Dave Perewitz of Cycle Fab. Shortly thereafter I rented by first shop and I've been on my own ever since.

Where do you get your ideas? Inspiration? You said you've got to come up with new stuff all the time.

I get some from MTV. Color choices sometimes I get from flannel shirts because they usually have a good variety of color and then a little fine detail of another color. I think you can get ideas from everything. You can walk down the street in

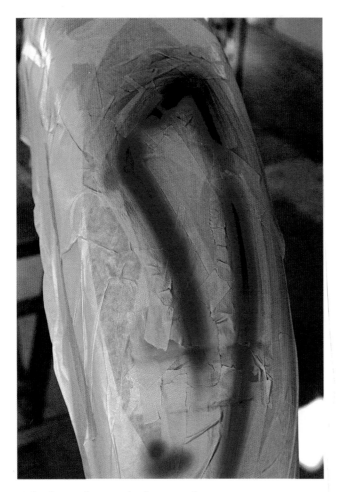

The last color, applied to another new area, is purple. Now it's time to pull the tape.

the middle of the city and get color ideas. I don't really limit myself to looking in magazines or other people's work. I really don't pay that much attention to what is going on out there already. I more or less just do what I do, and then working 16-18 hour days you really don't have a whole lot of choice.

Graphics are kind of a new thing. They've been out there, but no one has ever really taken advantage of them. As a matter of fact, I do get ideas...what I think are really raw ideas sometimes are the mini trucks and Volkswagens and stuff from California. I think those were adapted from radio control cars and trucks. They're geared toward young audiences to start up. They were geared toward 12 year olds, and mini trucks are definitely geared toward 25 and under. The ideas are really raw and not as refined usually, but still

very good. I like the applications and the color usage but it's usually a little scary for more conservative people.

Bobby Sullivan from Sullivan Brothers made the comment that he likes your stuff because it's not always the same.

Right. It's a real trick to try to constantly come up with new ideas. But if you're going to try to be on the forefront, you have to come up with new ideas all the time. You can't allow your idea-pool to stagnate. A lot of times when these bikes come out in the magazines, they were done six and eight months ago. So I'm always trying to produce new things because when they come out in the magazines, then whoever sees it in the magazine wants something just like what they just saw. But that work that they're seeing is work I did eight months ago.

The finished piece, before clearcoats are applied. Computer users could scan the original design and then use the plotter/cutter to actually cut the vinyl.

If you're not careful you could just keep reproducing your own stuff?

I won't. I won't reproduce the same thing. I never reproduce the same thing twice. Even if it's a variation, it's kind of like when you're working an idea through it brings you to the next place you're thinking of. The next little thought in your mind.

How much of your stuff is what people would call sign work?

That keeps changing, too. I would say less than 20% at this point. And even when it's sign work, it's fairly custom. Even the sign work, the spray painted signs, the lighted boxes I use House of Kolor materials. I don't use the paint that I'm supposed to use. The House of Kolor colors are more vibrant. Coming from museum school, from an art background, and dealing with mixing color from oil paint to acrylic paint - I absolutely fell in love with, at the time, Lacquers, because the candy colors were so pure.

The colors were so incredibly pure compared to what the regular oil paint was. You couldn't mix a purple in oil paint. You couldn't mix that kind of color. You'd have to get purple paint. But with this stuff you mix magenta and process blue and get this incredible purple. I was so shocked. I worked for Roy for a year. And one of the first days I worked there we were spraying some colors, and the masking paper was incredible, because the colors were so bright and clean, just the overspray. So I kind of fell in love at that point. I'm serious. It sounds so dramatic, but if you like color and you like paint you just can't help it.

Do you think the fine art background helps separate your stuff from other people's?

Yes. I'm very detail oriented. All the stuff I took when I studied fine arts was either a range from really abstract up to really fine detail, exact copies. I learned to copy the masters. At the art museum school, I went to the Museum of Fine Arts and had to copy paintings from the masters, so I learned a lot of techniques and I use a lot of those techniques with the candies and the pearls.

The biggest thing was getting used to using an airbrush as opposed to a brush. When you no longer have that hands-on it's really tough to adapt

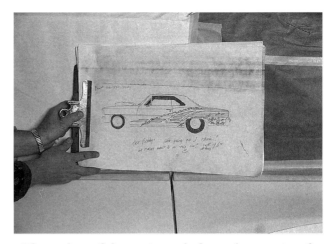

The outline of the car is made from photo copies of a side-view photograph, then create a design that fits the dimensions and proportions of the vehicle.

Nancy's first step is to scuff the shine off the paint with 500 grit paper and water, and then wipe the car down with wax and grease remover.

Nancy tapes the large piece of Transmask to the Chevelle. This masking material was marked and cut based on the paper pattern described in the text.

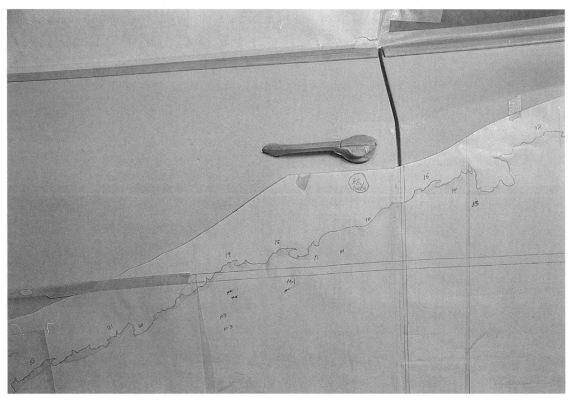

This close up shows how the body line and key hole are marked on the Gerbermask so it can be mounted with precision on the vehicle.

The large piece of masking tape across the paper acts as a hinge. Nancy will pull the backing off the top half, stick it to the car, squeegee the top half and repeat the procedure for the bottom.

the airbrush to fit with the things that you do by hand with a brush. It took me a long time to get used to that. The way that you do things is different, but the final result has to be somewhat the same. When you run tints and shadows and overlays and real transparent color over the surface, where you do it with a brush normally, now you've got to cut masks and take things off just to spray it. Whereas it would just be a stroke of a brush, and now it's a 20 minute process to do the same thing. You have to have a lot of patience to be able to do that.

Nancy peels the backing off the vinyl on the bottom half of the Gerbermask, next she carefully smoothes the vinyl over the sheet metal and works out bubbles with a squeegee.

Then you're working in all different size scales. You're working from 12 by 20 feet to little, tiny detail work on an air cleaner. You never really know. It's hard to keep the perspective straight, but it's kind of fun though. That's what gives it the variety. The bikes are the best because they're so detail oriented and you can finish them all off right down to a real fine detail whereas the big things like the trucks and everything you can't necessarily do that and still survive financially.

It's got to be really hard for the graphic artist like you, who only sees the bike or car as a series of pieces, to paint all those pieces and have everything line up.

You have to have a good memory of what the bike looks like. I do a lot of research. I go down there

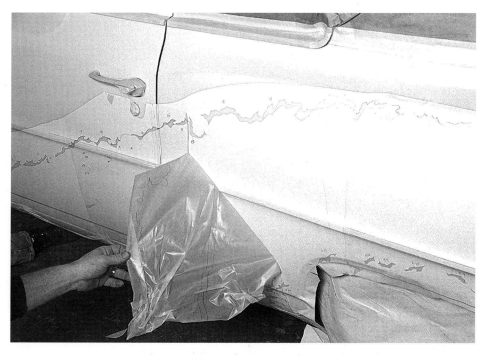

After the vinyl is stuck securely to the side of the Chevelle the transfer paper can be removed.

After the vinyl is in place it's time to mask off the rest of the vehicle - much easier than cleaning up overspray later.

As a good example of the detail that goes into one of these jobs, Nancy starts spraying the upper rip with blue blood red, applied with her Aztek airbrush. The blue blood red is part of the Shimrin, non-catalyzed, basecoat system.

and look at Dave's bikes or look at the bike that is going to be done. If they're stock bikes they're easy, but when they're all stretch tanks and all kinds of different things you really have to know how the layout is, how the level line of each piece is so you can match it through the whole process. That's one of those little tricks that you don't really think about too much until you're in the process of doing it. Which way does this fender really sit?

I understand you don't have a computer? You don't even cut your masks with a computer?

I hand cut everything. I've got seven people working for me, so having that kind of a production helps. Everybody learns it. Everybody is kind of apprentices at different stages.

So the vinyl cutting and all that computer generated Graphics haven't hurt you at all?

It's probably helped. It's reduced the competition. Everyone went toward the vinyl and I absolutely refused. All the old timers were saying, 'you've got to get a computer, the business is going that way, you've got to do it.' I got into this business because I liked the art part of it and I liked the color and the paint. I didn't get into it to cut vinyl. I stuck to my guns and took a lot of grief from a lot of people. It's been a hard road, and if you're talking about strictly making

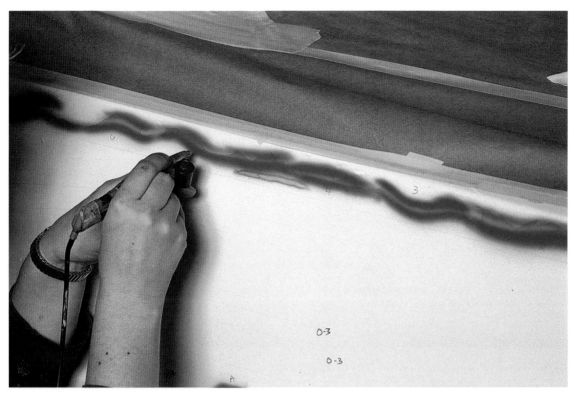

To "richen" the rip painted in blue blood red, Nancy comes back over the edges with kandy brandywine, mixed from Koncentrate and SG-100. Before she's finished with these rips, she will have added tangerine and deep purple.

After spraying the red rips and replacing the vinyl over those areas Nancy pulls the vinyl for the two spears seen above the rear wheel.

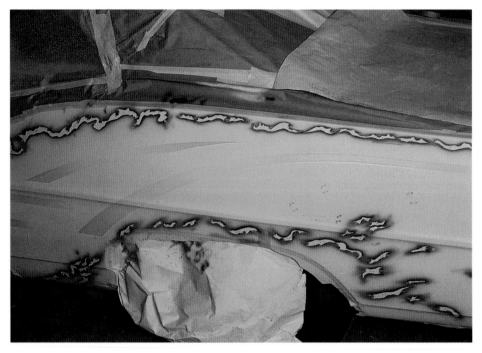

White basecoat is now applied to the center part of the two spears, followed by...

Black at the ends of the spears, followed by...

money you certainly make a lot more money doing the vinyl (per hour). I think the art background helps because I know how to draw, and it's always good to be able to put a picture in somewhere. People have incredible ideas, but they don't necessarily know how to put them down on paper.

So the raw idea is the customer's?

Yeah. They have an idea about what they want when they come in, or they saw another job they like and it gives me a point of reference to what they like. Then I talk to them for a half hour or however long it takes to determine what they want. They'll tell me what colors they like, what colors they don't like, the style that they like, the style that they don't like...we have lots of pictures here.

They'll come in with magazines or styles that they already have and then you develop it from there.

Is there one brand of airbrush that you like better than another?

Now I use these little Aztec plastic airbrushes. They're like Play School, like little toys. They're incredible. They weigh about an ounce. You don't have to hold the cup or anything. They do a good job and they're very light. They retail for about $100 so they're about the same as some of the other brushes. The tips are different, the whole design is completely different.

How much hand work do you do? By brush.

All the striping is done by brush. The lettering and stuff, quite a lot is still done by brush. A lot of the sub-copy is still done by brush and the outlining. Most of the things that get done are outlined, nothing we do here is left unfinished. We consider true craftsmanship of hand painting to be of the utmost importance.

A special mix of green (made up of Shimrin colors) in the center, where the white base was sprayed earlier.

This is our exit point, as the crew replaces the vinyl over the spears just painted in white, black and green. Now you begin to understand how and why people like Nancy Brooks have the reputation they do.

Chapter Five

The Fine Art of Airbrushing

Spray Painting In Miniature

Chapter One includes information on the airbrushes themselves. This chapter is meant to provide tips on use of the airbrush. Included here is both a start to finish sequence with Leah Begin, a very talented airbrush artist; and an interview with Jeremy Vecoli, educator and columnist. The interview is illustrated with a short series of exercises that Jeremy uses with his students, designed to help them understand how to best use their airbrushes.

The Devil's in the details - a thousand small colors, shapes and shadows - all of which define and create an airbrush image. The sequence that follows offers a *step-by-step examination of how one woman created this very life-like American Eagle.*

Airbrush Sequence at Let's Get Graphic.

This pure airbrush sequence is done at Let's Get Graphic by Leah Begin, who maintains her own company known appropriately as: Air It Is. During the three hour session Leah took time to explain both how she began using an airbrush and what she's learned in seven years of airbrushing everything from leather jackets to street rods.

Leah started out working on clothing and costumes. Her first airbrush designs were applied to those costumes and from there it was a short step to airbrushing leather jackets at biker events. When asked about the mistakes that first-time airbrushers make, Leah replied that most need to do more planning. "Not planning out their designs well enough is a major sin when you're starting. And they should be able to draw the subject with pencil and paper before trying to airbrush it - because you can only airbrush (freehand) as well as you can draw."

"I always drew things as a kid, but I never studied it hard in high school. When I started doing airbrushing on clothes I realized that I had allowed my drawing skills to slip, so I had to go back and re-learn those abilities."

Leah explains that she's always, "trying to get better with each design I do, there are more places I want to go. I think you can learn a lot by yourself. You have to find the material and always keep looking at what other artists do.

Before beginning on her Eagle, Leah studies various eagle images from books and magazines. On the left you can see the star stencils that will be used later.

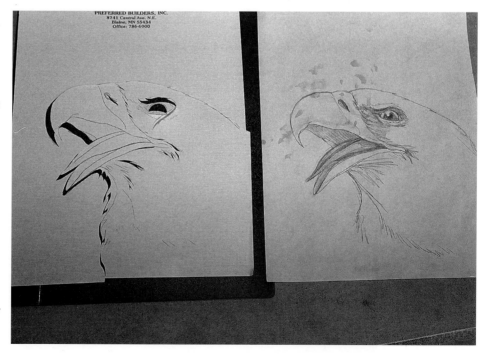

The stencil seen here is created from the original sketch over the light table. Parts of this stencil are hinged, so they can be pulled back as needed.

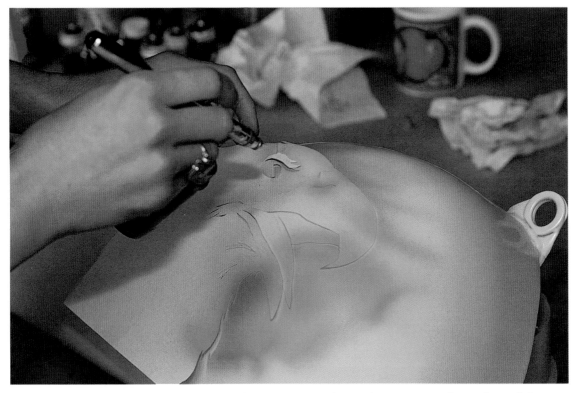

Here you can see how the overall image becomes a stencil to aid in creating the outline of the eagle's head. Most of the initial airbrushing is done in light purple, which will be darkened and shaded later in the process.

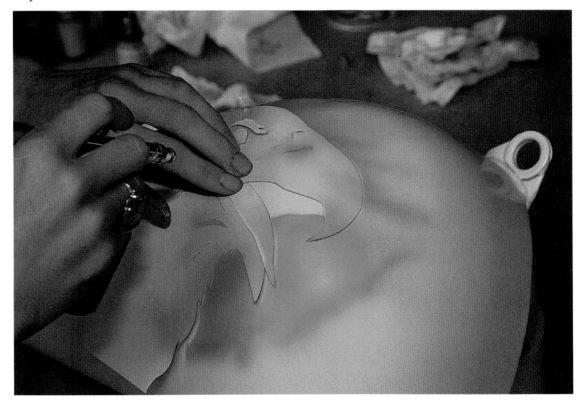

Close up shows how she begins to darken the area under the beak.

Leah does most of the work with an Omni model airbrush from Thayer & Chandler, though sometimes she uses the similar Vega. Both of which are run off the shop air at the relatively high pressure of 55 psi and sometimes more. Most of the paints used in this demonstration are PBC series pearls from House of Kolor, which Leah sometimes over-reduces slightly in order to help them spray easily with the airbrush.

The start of the project is a Harley-Davidson Fat Bob tank already painted with PC-5 prism pearl blue, which is nearly white and will make a good bright base under all the colors that follow. Leah starts by scuffing the tank before reaching for the airbrush.

In this case Leah starts with a sketch of the eagle's head she intends to put on the tank. With the sketch in hand she next goes to the light table where the original sketch is traced onto another sheet of paper. With an X-Acto knife she cuts the eagle's head out of this second-generation sketch. "I didn't cut through the design all the way," says Leah, "so I could peel parts of the design back or take them out later, like the flap at the eye or the area above the eye".

After the basic outline is painted in purple, PBC-65 passion pearl, Leah pulls the cut out and does some shadowing. Then she takes 901 cleaner to remove any adhesive left over from where the

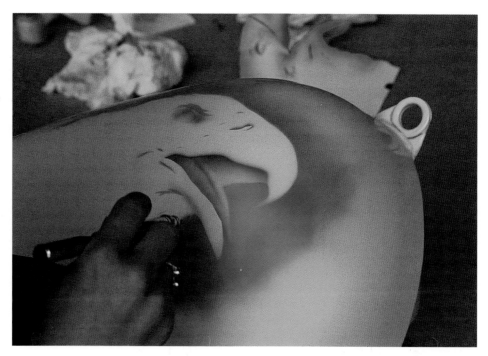

With the stencil removed It's time to begin creating the shadows and lines the will define the rest of the eagle's head

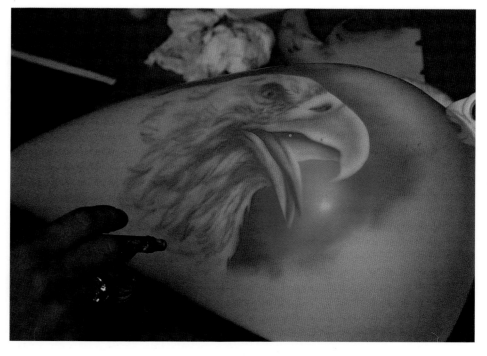

Now it's time to paint in the feathered texture on the neck. Note how shadow and highlight have been used to shape the beak and eye.

Working close to the tank with limited trigger pull Leah continues to build the eagle's head. The out-of-focus cloud beginning to form in front of the head will blend later with the flag background.

This is looking pretty good, and so far it's all in one color.

mask was first stuck to the tank.

Leah does the feathers under the beak freehand with the airbrush in the same purple used to do the outline, explaining as she does, "I like to use the purple for the first outlining because after I go over it with the yellow I get a nice warm brown color. "

"I do plan the jobs," says Leah, "but I like to leave some things open. That way I leave myself room to be creative." At this point Leah spends a considerable amount of time filling in details like the feathers on the neck of the bird. She adds some yellow at this point, a special-mix banana yellow color. With help from a stencil she adds this color to the beak and eyes, then begins adding yellow throughout the design and into the feathered sections.

Leah likes an airbrush with a lot of range, because it eliminates the need to use a lot of stencils.

Orange is the next color to be added, PBC-33 persimmon, to the tongue and mouth using the original cutout as a mask that she holds in place by hand. Next comes a special mix, a non-pearl red used to darken the tongue and mouth parts followed by more persimmon, which she uses lightly because it is a pearl and will reflect the light better that way.

Leah adds brown as a shadow under the upper beak, explaining as she does, "the hardest thing to learn about using an airbrush is patience. You have to stick with the design even when it irritates you."

Now she outlines some of the feathers with a light blue-grey to give them more depth, then a blue used to and darken the very front of the neck under the lower beak and the "clouds" out in front of the eagle's head. Now with a pearl red and help from a pre-cut mask she darkens the flag stripes, laying the red on over the purple put down earlier.

After applying the red she adds soft black lines running ninety degrees to the red and white stripes to create the "folds" in the flag and then softens the whole thing with more purple. Next she mixes up some special pearl white, (which is a mix of House of Kolor pearl white and BC-26 Shimrin white) and uses this special pearl white on the feathers, starting at the front of the neck under the beak. The white is also used to high-light the eye, and the feath-ers (she says it makes them fluffy) on the top and sides of the head. When working really close on details Leah almost touches the tank with the end of the airbrush.

At each color change Leah flushes the airbrush with reducer. When Leah sprays the stars with her home-made stencil she leaves one side, or one branch, of each star lighter than the others. She does this on purpose, "so the star

By using the stencil again and a mix of yellow paint Lead begins to color in the upper and lower part of the beak.

With the tongue part of the stencil pulled out of the way it's time to use red paint to darken the tongue and parts of the mouth.

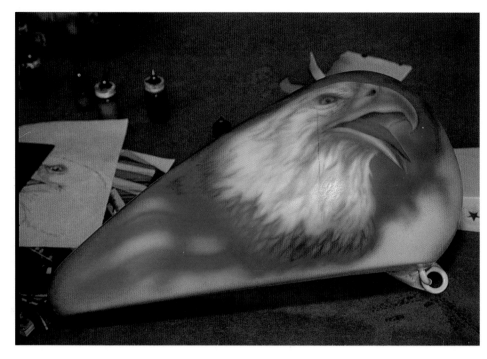

Some people might think the job looks nearly done at this point - but the real work has only begun.

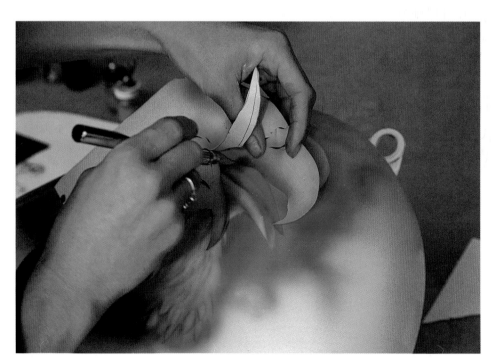

Here a mix of white is used to add highlights to the tongue which, in combination with the shadow down the center, really gives the tongue its shape.

looks out of focus, like it's moving. This way there's some motion in my little one-dimensional eagle." Then she fogs in more blue free hand to soften the edges of the stars.

With more special pearl white mix Leah adds highlights to the tongue, followed by a few more detail until she is satisfied with the end result.

What was only a sketch on paper three hours earlier is now a very well executed painting. All it took was two airbrushes, a variety of paints and reducers, plenty of patience and a skilled artist with over seven years of experience.

INTERVIEW, JEREMY VECOLI, AIRBRUSH ARTIST, . *In addition to this interview there are training exercises in this same chapter as well as a short hand brushing demonstration in Chapter Three. Though there are plenty of people who can use an airbrush, Jeremy is one of the few who really understand why an airbrush does what it does.*

Jeremy, why don't we start by asking how you got started in all this?

I was about 25 years old and had no real strong interest in art. I had seen a couple of airbrushes in hobby stores and was actually intrigued with them just because they were a neat looking mechanical device. I thought it'd be kind of neat to have one to play with. I had just quit my job as an automotive service writer and needed something to keep me busy. So I just started fooling around with one in my basement. I rented a couple of videos from an art supply store which really helped. Within two or three months, I managed to finagle my way into a local T-shirt airbrushing shop. This guy had been doing it for about 20 years. One thing that I thought was interesting was how little he could actually tell me about how it all worked, everybody that I had seen airbrushing seemed to be doing it very instinctively.

Nobody could explain what they were doing?

Exactly. I'm a slow learner and I have to understand something inside and out, three different ways, before I can go ahead and do it. I'm real analytical. I did martial arts for about 10 years and I was the same way learning that. But once I can do something, I can teach it to anybody because I really understand what is going on. After I'd been working at this T-shirt shop for a little under a year I managed to get hired at Six Flags Great America Theme Park in Chicago, airbrushing T-shirts there. I did that for three years.

After my second year at Six Flags, I had also been concurrently, in the off season, taking night school classes in sign painting just because that was something I

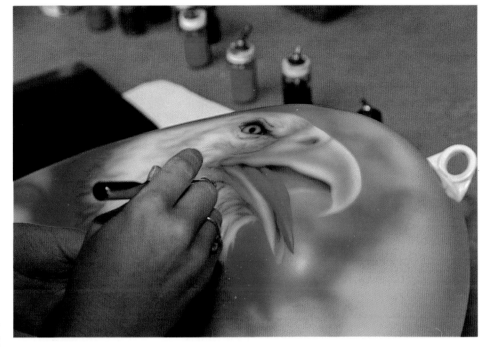

Brown is the color used at the edges of the beak, to create the shadow on the lower beak and under the upper beak.

All these stencils will be used in finishing the eagle's head - the Star stencils are cut by hand while the others are available from sign and art-supply houses.

had been exposed to and I thought it was interesting. I thought it would be a good thing to go along with my airbrushing because almost no airbrushers that I've seen know how to do sign lettering with a brush. I had found myself losing some work because of that. I realized that sign painting was an art to be admired. It was actually a very skilled trade. So I took some classes and went through their program pretty quickly. It's a night school program. On my instructor's recommendations the school hired me to teach an airbrush class, which I've done for three years now.

In fact, I developed their whole curriculum for teaching freehand airbrushing in the sign painting program. They had previously offered airbrushing in the commercial art program, but it was taught in a totally different way. Basically, it was taught using the "cut the stencil and spray in the hole" method that has been used since the turn of the century. Whereas the freehand T-shirt airbrushing method, which is also the exact same thing used for freehand illustrations on vehicles, was developed by people that had no formal graphic arts training.

People who were good free-hand airbrushers could do things that you never saw in an airbrush book, but most of them couldn't, or wouldn't, explain how. I had to invent some of the terminology used to teach the class because it's never really been taught in a large group. Most of the handouts that I made for the class I then sent right off to *Airbrush* magazine. They generally run my articles in every issue.

You're also a consultant for Badger airbrushes?

Yes, I met the president of Badger Airbrush. He was at Six Flags with his family. I talked with him and actually got invited to tour the factory. Just within the last year I've started traveling and

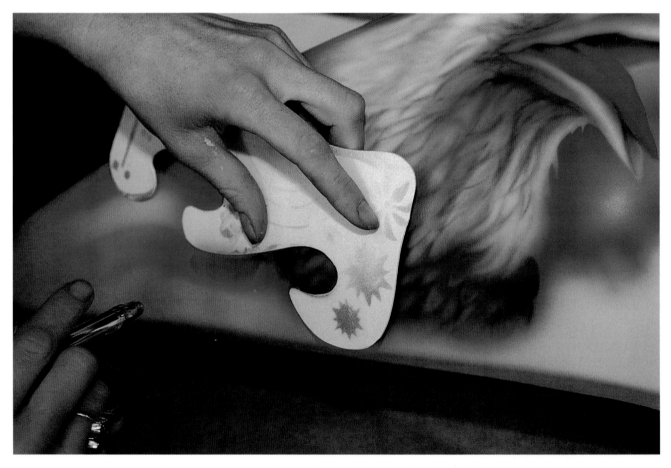

At this point Leah uses red paint and a stencil to make the stripes of the flag redder and darker.

doing seminars for them. I'm a part-time Artist/Consultant for Badger, I enjoy a good relationship with them. I work with them developing their new equipment and just wrote the instruction manual for their newest model that's coming out.

Do you want to cross over and talk some more about airbrushes? Can you tell me what makes a good airbrush for illustration on automobiles and motorcycles?

The biggest thing when you're selecting an airbrush is that it's not necessarily how much money you spend, but it's how smart you spend it. You have to know what kind of paint you're going to be using. Most automotive paint is going to be of the same consistency. A lot of this is knowing how to set your airbrush up for the kind of work you're doing. To start with you have to know how you're going to use the gun.

There are two kinds of airbrushes, a single-action and a double-action. The difference is that on a single-action when you press the trigger button down a preset amount of paint is immediately coming out and you can turn a knob on the back or front of the airbrush to set the amount of paint before you start painting. I prefer to use double action because it only costs a little more and the trigger controls both the paint and the air.

The finished stripes. Note how the wavy red stripes and black shadows reinforce the idea of folds in the flag.

Here you can see how light blue-gray was used to give depth and detail to the feathers on the neck, and how the clouds in front of the bird have taken on a darker blue hue.

Pearl white is used to further detail the feathers under the beak, note how close the airbrush is to the tank during detail work like this.

Working with a white pearl, Leah works to give the feathers a "fluffy" and life-like appearance.

So the double-action works like a full-size spray gun?

It does, but it has a much longer stroke on the trigger. The airbrush needle has a long fine taper on it, so there's a lot of area "in between" wide open and fully shut. Most production spray guns have such an abrupt taper on the needle that it's either on or off. An airbrush can do everything in between, and all you have to do is be comfortable with the airbrush so you always know how much paint is going to come out at any given trigger position.

In terms of automotive type work what do you need in an airbrush?

You don't need anything really fancy. There are a couple different kinds of airbrushes. Some that use jars to hold the paint with a siphon straw that goes into the jar. The siphon straw sucks up the paint. There are others that have little tiny cups on top of the airbrush that you use an eye dropper to fill, for working in tight areas or using very small amounts of paint. And there are airbrushes that can be converted to work both ways, which have just come out and are kind of interesting.

In terms of the chemicals that are in automotive paints, is there anything special you have to worry about?

Not at all. Just remember to clean your airbrush by spraying an appropriate solvent through it when you're done. Airbrushes are usually made out of chrome plated brass and are going to be impervious to chemicals. Any kind of paint that you can thin down enough to get it to spray can go through an airbrush whether it's lacquer, urethane or whatever.

No trouble with O-rings dissolving in the solvents?

Not really, depending on the make and model. Some airbrushes are designed with very tight tolerances that have no plastic or rubber seals. Some of the ones I use have Teflon seals which aren't going to react to anything. Most airbrushes are very low maintenance if you keep them clean. They have about the same number of moving parts as a ball-point pen. The first thing I do with my students is make them take the airbrush apart and put it back together a few times. It's like field stripping a rifle. Just so they're not scared. It's just a tool. I still have my first one and it works great. It's five years old and I beat it. Parts are usually very easy to replace. You can usually get replacement parts wherever you got your airbrush.

Do some airbrushes have more range than others?

Yes. A lot of it again is set up. Some airbrushes have different size tip and needle combinations which allow them to spray a wider variety of paints. One common myth about airbrushes that everybody seems to

have is that if you have an airbrush with fine, medium, and heavy duty tips, they think it's to make fine lines, medium lines, or wide spray. In actuality, you should match your tip and needle size to the thickness of the paint you're using.

If you're using a real runny ink or dye use your

The white color is used on and around the eye to detail the feathers there, and give the eye a certain luminance.

fine tip and needle combination, which has a much smaller opening. If you're using heavy pottery glaze use your large tip and needle which has a large opening. That way' you'll always get the same spray pattern and a predictable response no matter what thickness paint you're using. If you run a thin ink or dye through a large nozzle opening, it's just going to act like a fire hose the minute the trigger is pulled back more than a quarter of the way. You want to match it so you get a nice steady spray throughout the whole range of trigger travel.

Are there some that require changing tips and needles whereas others might be able to cover the same range without changing tips?

There are airbrushes out there that go with a happy medium. Those generally work fine for automotive paints. Generally, they're designed to use a paint that's been thinned to about the con-sistency of milk. Whereas if you're using an illustration dye, which is very thin, like water, that would go through an airbrush a lot faster. You want to use a smaller tip to control that. The one-size-fits-all airbrushes have just come out in the last year or two really. I always use medium tips on my airbrushes, except for a couple of my illustration airbrushes for when I'm doing super-fine detail.

Are the compressors a big deal in terms of the amount of air and the quality of the air itself?

Quality of air is important especially for moisture control. It's usually when you're working very close on a detailed project that a shot of water comes through. You don't need nearly as much air pressure as you would with a touch-up gun or a regular full size gun. A lot of it depends on the type of airbrush. Some airbrushes aren't very efficient suction wise, they don't suck the paint up

More highlights in white help to give these feathers depth.

very well. You might have to run up to 70 or 80 pounds of pressure to get them to spray right. Whereas you can take another airbrush and use 35 pounds and it will have the exact same amount of suction at the straw (the siphon tube) as the other one.

I actually ran a test with a mercury suction gauge on several different airbrushes. I kept turning up the air pressure until the suction didn't change. And once you determine what that pressure is for your airbrush, turning up the air pressure won't increase the suction - it will only increase your overspray. I prefer to use what I would term a high-suction airbrush where I can get the paint going through the brush with less air pressure. Everything works a little more smoothly. I get a little more control. There are certain brands I prefer.

Back to the air. A moisture trap on the air hose is a good idea?

Yes. Generally you're going to be working with anywhere from 15 to 65 pounds of pressure. And maybe even a cubic foot per minute of air. It's negligible. I use a small 3/4 horsepower compressor with tank. It kicks in every once in a while when I'm going full blast. Any kind of compressor will work. There are silent compressors, made especially for airbrushing, that use air conditioner pumps. They're absolutely quiet, but they have a short

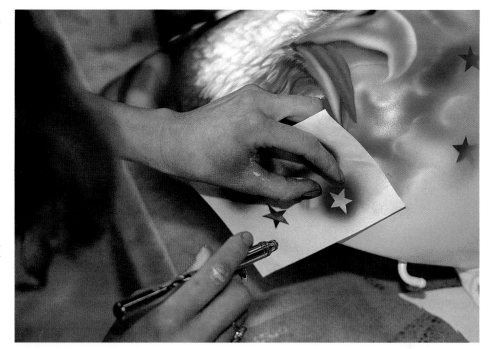

Here you see the star stencil being used with blue paint and how one side is left light on purpose so it seems to blend into the cloud.

Purple, shading to blue with white highlights, creates a very realistic set of clouds on the front of the tank. Stars fading to blue work with the flag and eagle theme.

life span and they're expensive. People should try to keep the moisture trap closer to the airbrush than to the compressor. This allows the air to cool somewhat resulting in better moisture separation.

You also have the option of using a carbon dioxide or nitrogen tank, one you can get from any welding supply place. All you have to buy is a regulator and then you just rent the tanks.

And I suppose there's no moisture in there either?

Not in the nitrogen. Carbon dioxide can frost up. If you're painting a lot of high volume stuff it'll be more of a problem. If you're just doing a motorcycle tank here and there, that's a lot different than doing 100 T-shirts on a busy Saturday. A 50 pound carbon dioxide tank will go a long time. Two full-time busy T-shirt artists can go a whole weekend on one of the big five foot tall nitrogen tanks.

In terms of the usage, do people make a lot of

mistakes? What about when they set up the gun when it's brand new?

The big thing is knowing what to expect and understanding what the airbrush can and can't do. That gives you a real good indicator right away if something's not working right. You need to have an understanding of what sort of control is achievable. That's the whole emphasis of my freehand airbrushing class that I teach. I don't make people artists. I don't teach people to draw. You can use those abilities and then take an airbrush and combine it with whatever visual skills you have.

Freehand airbrushing is a *motion* art. It's not a visual art. It's like learning karate. The visual art part of it, to me, is kind of an incidental by-product. A lot of it is learning how to move your hands and your trigger instinctively while you're only concentrating on what you're painting. Especially when I'm doing lettering, I can't think about: do I

The top of the tank shows the full flag effect with stars done in a reverse.

pull the trigger back a little or a lot, how high do I make this line, is this one going to be thick or thin, oh yeah, what letter comes next? You can see how it would really start to overwhelm you. You drill a lot of it into your subconscious through training, not learning. It's like learning to juggle. The process happens faster than you can think. So you find elements that are constantly repeating themselves and you train those down to a subconscious level. That's the only way you can really do it.

Especially with lettering there are a lot of things you have to remind yourself to do when you're airbrushing. Like always having the air come on first and then bringing up the appropriate amount of paint, instead of pulling the trigger back and then hitting the air and getting an abrupt blast of paint which might be more than you wanted. You have to just practice and train until you're not really thinking about it. Then you have your mind free to concentrate on what kind of job you actually want to do. It's really important because a lot of it happens kind of fast sometimes.

When you think about it that way and you kind of understand what you're up against, then usually the learning process will go faster and it's not nearly as discouraging.

Leah Begin has little formal art training. She cites the study of other artists and her own patience (and talent) as the key to her success.

The finished bird, before clearcoating. Though it looks easy in the sequences, a thousand small decisions and details are what really make this a great design.

83

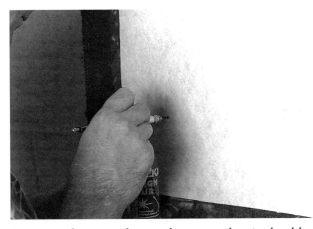

To start, the tip is close to the paper, the air should come on first, then the trigger is pulled back slightly to create one little dot. Then the trigger goes forward so the paint flow will stop while leaving the air on.

Without turning the air off, you have to move the gun over, and farther away from the paper, then turn the paint back on for the next dot.

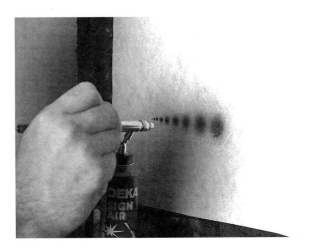

To make bigger dots, the gun moves farther away from the paper and the trigger is pulled just a little farther back.

So if you broke down the first part of the learning process into sub parts what would they be?

One of the most important things is learning how to get the air coming on with no paint, which is simply pushing down the trigger but not pulling it back.

Then slowly pulling back the trigger and watching how your spot of paint on your surface will grow and when it's at the size you want, you don't pull the trigger back anymore. It's a matter of training a reaction into your hand to stop your finger moving when you like what you see. It does not have a mind of its own. An airbrush is a great tool and it can help you a lot, but you can't look at the ceiling and start spraying and be happy with what you get.

The compliment to that is to always push your trigger forward while you still have air going through the gun, before your shut off your air by lifting up the trigger. If you have your trigger held back and then just lift up on the air, you still have probably a drop of paint hanging on the end of the needle. Then when you go hit your air, even if the trigger is all the way forward and no paint's supposed to come out, a little blast will come out.

You've got to shut off the paint before you shut off the air and turn on the air before you start bringing the paint out.

The rest of it is learning how to move your hand?

Yes. There's a lot of things that go into that. There's a whole area of body mechanics that I don't really think has been expressed well in the art field, but it's fairly well understood in a lot of other areas. I've done a lot of martial arts and have had formal pistol shooting instruction and a lot of that helped. The biggest thing is most people literally do not know how to draw because the most experience they have holding something in their hand and making marks is writing. And drawing is the opposite if you want to get technical. When you write, you anchor the palm of your hand flat on a surface and you move your fingers. When you draw, you anchor your fingers and move your entire hand.

I prefer to do freehand airbrushing standing up, because in some cases you can get more control by anchoring your arms at your sides and shifting your weight from one foot to the other. You can actually get very fine control that way. One of the other big things - this is again based on a handout from my class on body mechanics for airbrushing - is optical leading, something that has been totally ignored in airbrushing. This means that if you look ahead of your hand your hand will move to where you're looking. If you're looking at your hand, you aren't giving it any useful guidance.

It's hard with airbrushers, especially because it's so fascinating to watch this invisible ray of paint suddenly appear when it hits the surface. You end up watching that, and if you're trying to make a smooth line it doesn't work. It's like trying to drive a car looking at the road two feet in front of you, you end up making abrupt steering corrections all the time. You can train yourself, but it's a little disconcerting at first, to be looking not at where you're at, but where you want to go.

I have drills for my students where I have them draw a circle with an airbrush and end up where they started. It is a good way to learn control. If it's done properly you can't tell the starting and stopping points. Penciling a shape and then following that line with the airbrush has twice the benefit because now you have an

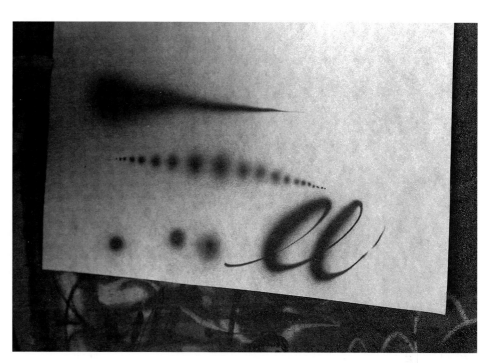

These are all good exercises for the beginning airbrush artist. After increasing the size of the dots the process is reversed, all to train your trigger finger and your brain.

Here we have a "rat's tail," another good exercise that trains the artist to move the gun closer to the paper and reduce the flow of paint, all while moving the airbrush from left to right.

85

Jeremy is constantly cleaning any accumulations of paint off the tip of the needle.

element of accountability added in where you have to stay on a line. Students hate it because suddenly they have something they can be judged against. But you can use that as a self-correcting guidance to help yourself learn faster.

So you have to have technical skill and whatever art abilities you posses.

It's basically the ability to really see something and then recreate it. A lot of airbrushers are concentrating on the special effects they can do. Most airbrushers really aren't good artists, myself included.

The basic "rat's tail" can be combined in various forms, sometimes with a soft dot in the center, to create these simple but pleasing shapes.

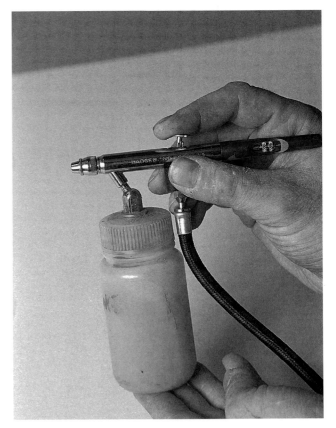

Note the way the airbrush is cradled in the right hand. This will provide optimal control. The left hand under the jar was used only to steady the airbrush for the photo.

Going back to how this whole thing started in my class, I teach techniques that teach them how much control they can get out of an airbrush. What they do with that is up to them. My class is useful for people with all sorts of different ranges of interests. Everybody is in my class for a different reason. Basically I teach them, 'You can make your airbrush do this, this, and this.' This is how you train yourself to be able to get the most out of it. It's like buying an expensive racing motorcycle. Most guys just want to go down to the lake and pick up girls, they don't really understand the machine or utilize its full abilities.

Do you need to be a technician before you're an artist?

I think so. It will help you execute whatever you have brewing in your mind to its fullest

Hot pink provides most of the color for the body of the flames.

A simple set of flames is created by first drawing them out and then cutting a stencil. Red-orange is used at the tip of the flames.

potential. There are people who have technical skill without a lot of artistic skill. They will make more money than the people who have the artistic vision but don't have the technical skill to bring it out. I'm certainly not an inspired artist, but I can be given a task and execute it in a manner that will be acceptable to my customer.

People always complain that airbrushes spit? Why do they spit?

Due to poor maintenance generally or trying to run a paint that is too thick for the type of airbrush. If I'm having a problem like that the first thing I'll do is try to spray some water or appropriate solvent through the brush. Sometimes there can be bits of dried paint in the airbrush. If you're using poorly filtered paint you'll get intermittent clogs that then eject themselves through the nozzle opening. My airbrushes don't spit.

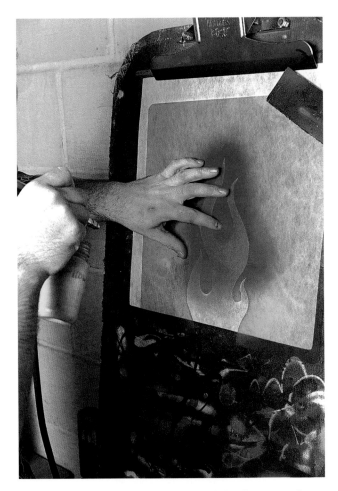

Now yellow is used for the base of the flames and blended smoothly into the hot pink.

So it's user failure?

A lot of it is the user not understanding what is happening in their airbrush and letting paint dry inside it. I use jar-fed airbrushes with jars that attach to the bottom of the brush. I generally store my airbrushes on a full jar so the end of the siphon straw is under water so to speak, and I make sure the needle is all the way forward in the nozzle. That way nothing can dry inside the airbrush. A person who takes their airbrush off the jar and sets the airbrush on the counter will have trouble. You need to have an understanding relationship with your equipment and realize the consequences of what you do.

A final word of advice for beginners in terms of mistakes you see people make, or advice that they don't get but should?

The biggest problem I see with my students is

you can use an airbrush to make hard edges or soft faded techniques, and their hard lines are generally too soft and their soft effects are generally too hard and they end up looking the same. The biggest thing you can do to make yourself use your fullest potential is to understand how the paint comes out of the airbrush and how it hits the surface. Learn what's going to happen when you work at different distances and don't be scared to make a few mistakes.

Learn that for every trigger position there's also a matching distance away from the work surface that will get you the best results, nice even coverage without runs or spots where paint didn't hit. If you're working with just a little bit of paint coming out with the trigger barely pulled back, you are also going to work close to the surface. It's almost like a focal point, where the spray is in proper

By putting the stencil back in place and applying a contrasting violet Jeremy creates more contrast for the flame design.

focus. It's a cone-shaped spray, there's a cross section where everything is happening right and you have to discover that through practice.

As you pull the trigger back farther that focal point gets farther away from the tip of the gun At a given trigger pull the dot will be a given size. Then you can adjust the softness and hardness of the line by the distance between the airbrush and the object.

You also have to remember that a nonabsorbent surface is going to require more finesse than spraying a T-shirt where you can really soak the paint on and it's not going to run and drip all over. That's why scuffing your surface, if you're doing automotive work, will definitely make your life easier because that surface will grab hold of the paint.

Are there any other exercises like you talked about following the circle?

There's an exercise that's called the dot drill that is taught to train trigger position awareness. Basically you're making a row of dots next to each other that progressively get larger and larger and then smaller and smaller, from a pinpoint to about the size of a penny. You keep the air on the whole time, so you're automatically learning to leave your air on and use the back and forth motion of your trigger to meter your paint. You don't interrupt the air to stop it. You are learning to get accustomed to how much paint is going to come out at any given position. You're learning this by what you feel, your perception of how far back you've pulled the trigger versus what you see on your work surface because you can't really look at your airbrush while you're doing it.

It's hard when you're doing script lettering with an airbrush, because you'll pull the trigger all the way back for your fat down stroke and then you will push it almost all the way forward when you're going up, so it's a nice skinny line. Your finger has to remember how far it can go without cutting off the paint entirely and causing an interruption in the line. That comes through what is called muscle memory. The more you can do that and just instinctively know what's going to hap-

The final photo, multi-colored flames, with contrasting violet outline, done in a fast, simple fashion.

pen, the better your airbrushing is going to look. Freehand airbrushing especially does not look good if it's done slowly and carefully. It's better if it's done correctly and confidently at a nice working pace.

You get lines to flow nicer and the whole design flows better?

Exactly. Lettering with a paint brush you can go a little slower. You can freeze and nothing will happen. If you freeze with paint constantly coming out of your airbrush, you're going to have a problem. The biggest thing I ran into in learning sign lettering was, "Hey, you can slow down". That was actually pretty neat I thought.

Chapter Six

Hands On

Flames, Fades and Signs

This first of the Hands-On chapters includes a wide variety of work. First is a set of non-conventional flames applied to a set of Harley-Davidson sheet metal with the new Kameleon paints. Sequence number two is a multi-layer graphic and

includes airbrush, lettering brush and pinstriping work. We like to think there is something here for everyone, no matter what your interests or current level of experience.

SEQUENCE NUMBER ONE:

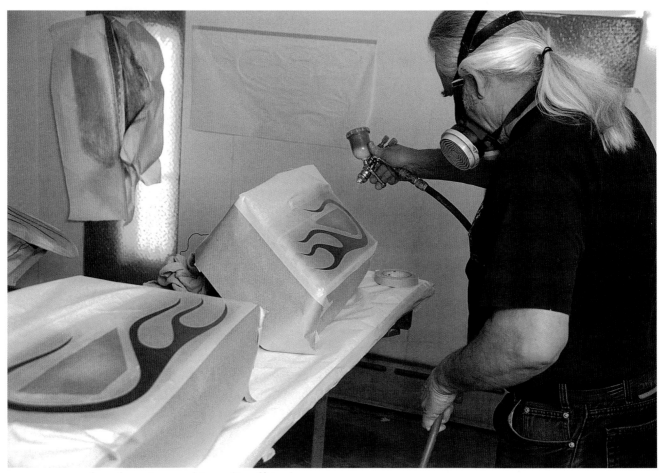

sequence number three is a multi-media affair that

Here we see Jon Kosmoski as he creates an unusual set of flames with the new Kameleon color-change paint.

90

Drag Bags at House of Kolor

This Harley-Davidson Dresser being painted with flames belongs to one of the employees of Drag Specialties, manufacturer and distributor of aftermarket parts. The flames are laid down on a base color done with three coats of PBC-103 cortez blue pearl sprayed over BC-25 Shimrin black. Next we applied three coats of UC-1 clear (because we don't ever want to sand on the pearl), waited for the final coat to dry, and then scuffed the clear with 500 grit sandpaper. This clear should be allowed to dry for at least 12 hours at a minimum temperature of 70 degrees. Painters have trouble in the winter because they spray the final coat of clear, turn down the heat in the shop and go home, expecting the clear to be fully cured the next day, even though the shop cooled to well below 70 degrees during the night.

After trying one design on the bag we make a template with masking paper. This will serve as a reference if the bike's owner decides to use that design. Then we try another design just to see which one we like better. The beauty of using tape for the layout versus some of the liquid mask systems is that you can change the design as many times as you want. The tape in this case is 1/8 inch Scotch Pressure Sensitive tape designed for professional auto refinishing (this is regular masking tape, sometimes called crepe tape). The fact that this tape may leave a slightly soft edge isn't important because the flames will be pinstriped when we finish. After completing a second flame design we make a template of that and then hang the two flame designs side by side on the wall for comparison.

Once the customer approves one of the designs we run the pounce wheel over that design from the back side, then sand the paper nibs off the paper with 180 grit sand paper. Next we tape the pounced pattern on the saddle bag and then pound the pounce pad gently against the paper. After pulling the paper the correct pattern can be seen as an outline made up of pounce dust.

Before doing the actual tapeouts we make sure the location of the design is the same on both

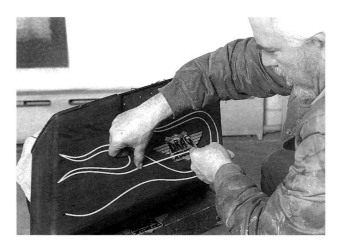

For this set of flames we tried two different layouts before deciding which one we, and the customer, like best.

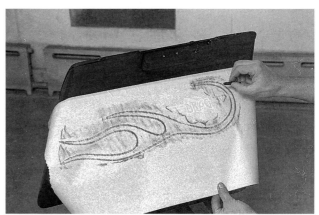

We saved each of our designs by running charcoal over the paper that over-lays the tape. The nice thing about using tape is that if you don't like it, all you have to do is pull the tape and start over.

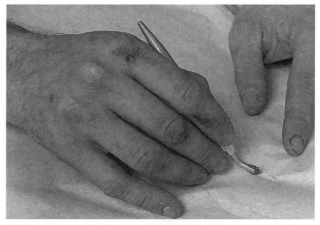

The pounce wheel is a good low-tech way to repeat a design. Just run the wheel over the paper, with the paper lying on a soft surface, then use the pounce chalk to leave an outline of the design.

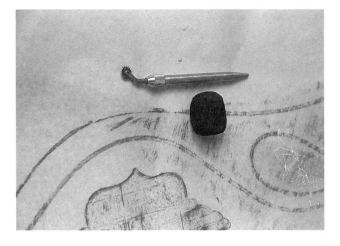

Tools of the trade, a pounce wheel, available from any good sign or art-supply store, and a piece of chalk.

The pounce pad is like a sponge for the dark powder, when it's gently tapped against the ventilated paper a tell-tale line of pounce dust is left behind.

bags. We begin taping out the pattern with 1/8th inch masking tape after first blowing off the excess "dust," because too much of it will inhibit the adhesion of the tape. For the mask of the gas tank, we only try to get the paper to wrap around the main part of the tank, because it's so hard to get the paper to conform to the curves of the tank.

Note: before doing the tape layout on the bags or another part of the bike we carefully wash the surface with soapy water. The clearcoat has already been scuffed with 500 grit paper to knock down the shine and improve adhesion of the flame paint.

Back to the bags, we buy some two layer vinyl materi-al, Gerbermask, with light

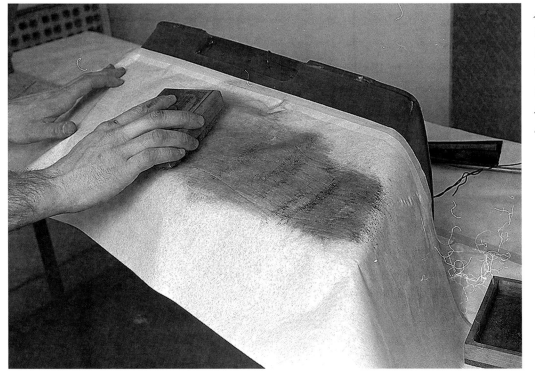

After the small nibs have been sanded off the backside of the paper we taped the paper to the bag and "pounced," it by slapping the pounce pad against the paper.

adhesive on the back side (the same material seen earlier in the book). Once we have the vinyl the layout goes like this:

1. Cut a piece of Gerbermask.

2. Lay the Drag logo on it, tape it in place with tape on the back side.

3. Spray the edge with an airbrush. Use a color that will contrast with the object you're going to stick this to.

4. Cut out the mask along the outline left by the paint (if this sounds confusing check the photo for a better understanding).

5. Peel off the backing from the Gerbermask and stick the mask of the logo in place on the two bags. We are going to use the Kameleon paint in this logo area, normally I use a black base under the new paint but because the deep purple is so dark we decide to simply spray the Blue-to-Cyan Kameleon paint right over the purple.

6. With the cutout in place I spray 3 light coats of the color-change paint, waiting for flash times between each coat. For this job I use a small Binks HVLP touch up gun.

7. After the final coat of kameleon paint has dried (usually around five minutes) I apply one coat of SG-100 intercoat clear to protect the paint.

Now we mask off the rest of the flames on all the sheet metal, tack the area lightly and then apply three coats of red-to-gold color-change paint with the same

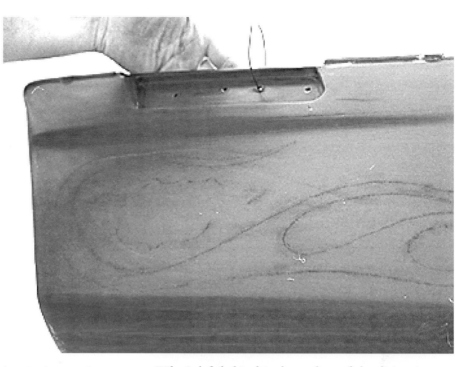

What's left behind is the outline of the design in pounce dust. We like to blow off the excess before we start taping.

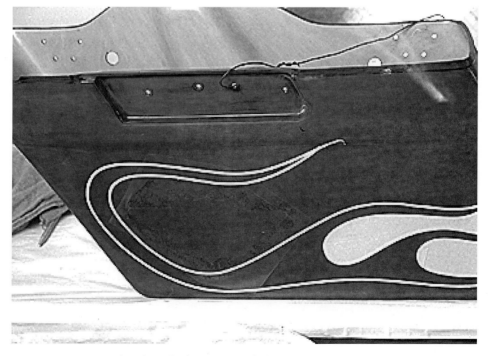

Now we can go ahead with the taping of all the parts. All of this was done with crepe tape, or conventional masking tape.

The Drag Specialties logo will be re-created by first making an outline of a logo decal from some masking material.

After being cutout, and the backing removed, the mask or stencil (which is hard to see here) is stuck to the bag.

You can see here we have masked off the rest of the saddle bag prior to application of the Kameleon paint.

small Binks HVLP gun used earlier. I should note that we mixed the color change paints at double the normal reduction before I applied four light coats of the red-to-gold paint. At the tips of the flames I add a second color, a special green-to-purple flip flop shade applied with another touch up gun, this one from DeVilbiss.

What's left is to pull the tape and apply final clear. When pulling the tape there are a few things I like to emphasize. The tape should have been applied so it comes off easily and in large pieces - what went on last should come off first. Pull the stripping tape last and be sure to pull all the tape directly away from the paint so you're less likely to have it pick up the edge of the paint. Once the tape is off I like to run a dull knife blade over the tape edge to knock it down, so it takes fewer coats of clear to create that smooth surface we're looking for.

Once the tape is off we wash the surfaces with Ivory dish soap and a white Scotch Brite pad. You have to be sure the water runs over the entire surface, if it is repelled in one area that spot isn't clean and the paint probably won't stick there, or it might fish-eye.

For clear we applied four coats of UC-1, our fastest curing clear, mixed with 310, our fastest drying reducer. I apply a light bond coat first, followed by three heavier coats and let this dry for a minimum of 12 hours at seventy degrees.

Note: Turn to Chapter Three to see how these parts were pinstriped and how the logo was recreated based on the silhouette shape painted here with the Kameleon paint. Following the application of the pinstripes we do the final application of clear, UFC-1 in this case.

SEQUENCE NUMBER TWO:

Nancy Brooks puts Graphics on a Motorcycle fender.

In this sequence we follow along as Nancy Brooks puts the graphics on the fender of a David Perewitz Road King. This is the second time Nancy has put the graphics on this fender, the job seen here is a recreation of the original graphics, made necessary by a small accident. So the other fender you see in the background of some photos is the original front fender which Nancy keeps nearby for comparison.

At this point the logo has been sprayed, coated with SG-100 and taped over. We're nearly ready to spray the Kameleon paint in the flamed areas.

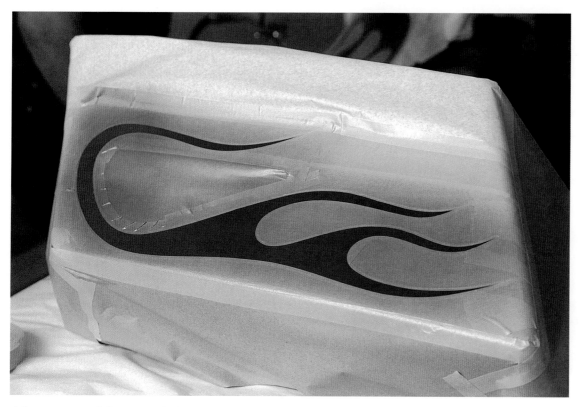

The paint used for most of the flames is red-to-gold Kameleon (sometimes called flip-flop paint for the way it changes color so dramatically depending on the light source and direction).

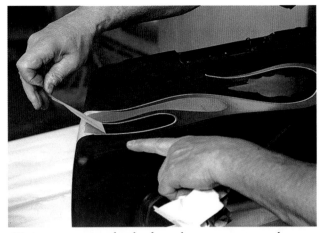

It's important to think about how you put on the tape - so that when it comes time to pull it off it comes off easily, in large chunks.

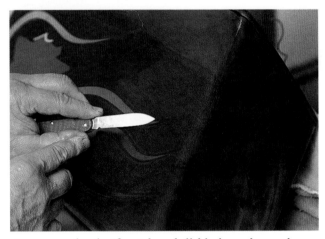

I use a pocket knife with a dull blade and run the edge of the blade over the edge where the paint met the tape. The paint likes to climb that edge, the knife blade is a good way to knock it down.

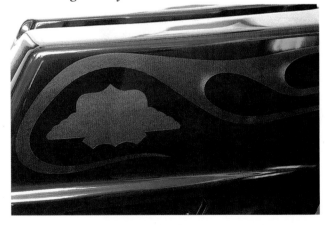

This is the finished saddle bag, after pulling the tape, washing the surface and applying four coats of UC-1 clear.

As always, Nancy starts the project with a sketch, which she soon takes to the light table. A two-layer piece of Transmask is taped over the sketch, so she can see the sketch showing through. Now she cuts the design out on the vinyl.

Nancy explains that, " all the layers of the design have to be cut out and the pieces removed separately, like a jigsaw puzzle. Then the pieces will have to be stuck down again. How hard a certain piece will be to put back down is part of the overall layout decision. Removal and replacement of these puzzle pieces should be done carefully so as not to distort or stretch them."

After cutting out the design on the vinyl, she puts down the transfer tape, then trims the piece and positions it on the fender. The mask is attached to the fender in a "hinged" fashion, so Nancy can fold back one half, pull out the backing from the backside of the Transmask, stick down that half, then fold back the other half and repeat the procedure.

Next, she masks off the rest of the fender and applies the first color to the upper and central parts of the fender. This color is blue blood red applied with a touch up gun. After the red is dry Nancy puts the 'cut out' sections back down to mask the area that was just painted blue blood red.

Now Nancy takes the masking paper off the lower part of the fender and gets ready to paint the large overlapping triangles. The first coat is a white base, BC-25 followed by a mixture of snow white pearl PBC-44, and sunrise pearl PBC-30. Next comes sunrise pearl blended over the lighter mixture applied just minutes before. When doing blends Nancy likes to work from light to dark.

Then parts of the same area are further blended with a mixture of snow white and tangelo. In this case Nancy is trying to match the job done earlier, which is tough considering that she doesn't always keep notes and almost always works from a mixture not a straight color.

Next the "lines" of candy tangerine which will help to separate the visual layers are added. Now Nancy puts down all the old "triangle" masks and pulls the vinyl on the upper pieces and base coats those. Purple is the next color to be applied (another Nancy-Brooks special mixture), to one of the spears above the taillight. Orion silver, which Nancy likes because it has relatively large flakes, is used for the long slim spear that runs through the triangles.

Now Nancy pulls the masks off the inner section of each triangle and sprays the inner triangles with white and black - this is base for the teal that will follow. White and black are blended with an eye to the way they will affect the final color of the teal that will follow.

The teal is now sprayed on the inner triangles, with white highlights added next. A gravel texture for parts of the vertical spears is created by first using black, with silver dabbed in, then fuscia, then air brush on a light teal, followed by airbrush application of a darker teal.

After removing the backing from the masking material so it adheres to the fender Nancy pulls off the transfer paper.

Finally it's time to remove the vinyl mask. The fender will still have to be clearcoated with three coats of clear, watersanded and then pinstriped (see Chapter Four) and then clearcoated another six to nine coats before it is sanded and buffed.

SEQUENCE NUMBER THREE:

Norm's Tire sign by Lenni Schwartz from Krazy Kolors.

At first glance this might seem like a simple sign job done on a company pickup truck. What's interesting, however, is the way Lenni uses airbrush, hand lettering and pinstriping to create the design for Norm's Tire in Little Canada, Minnesota.

As usual the first step is cleaning with Gon wax and grease remover. If there's any doubt about whether or not the vehicle is really clean Lenni starts the process with soap and water (which

Nancy does all her cutting by hand on the light table. Here she has the sketch positioned under the masking material.

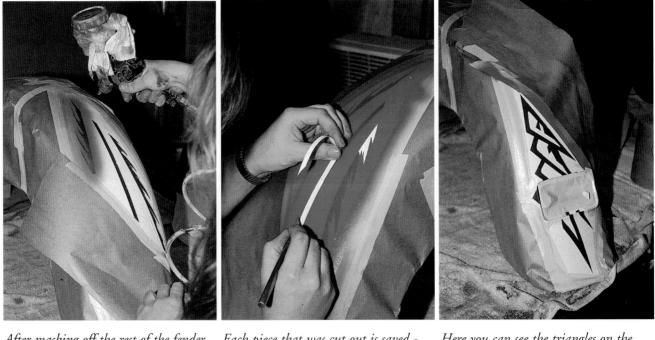

After masking off the rest of the fender, Nancy puts down the blue blood red

Each piece that was cut out is saved - so it can be used later to re-mask the areas that were just painted.

Here you can see the triangles on the lower part of the fender before application of basecoat.

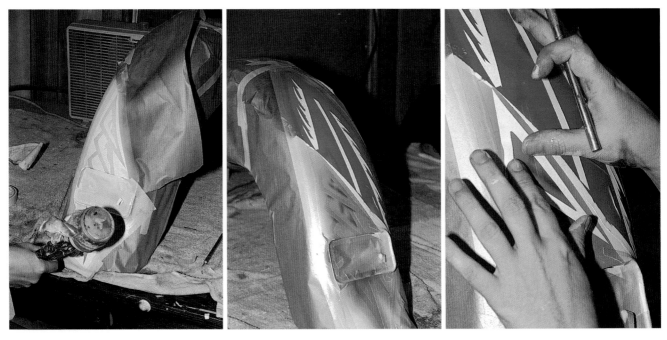

A white basecoat is used under the triangles on the lower fender.

Here we see the triangles after the final blending and application of paint.

Again, the triangles shaped pieces of vinyl are used to mask off the area that was just painted.

removes some materials that solvents like Gon won't) followed by wax and grease remover.

Before the painting can start Lenni runs a piece of guide tape just under the upper body line, followed by two pieces of tape just slightly lower that will form the border for the actual pinstripes.

Part of the design includes the sign running along the bottom of the door. For this Lenni measured the truck earlier and then cut a mask from Gerbermask material on the computer-driven cutter back at the shop. Now he needs only make sure the mask is positioned properly by marking parallel lines on the door that will act as a placement guides. The lines are made with a Stabilo pencil, and even though the it's water soluble Lenni likes to keep the lines as light as possible.

Though the Tire Sales letters were cut on the

As you see here the basecoats for the teal is made up of light and dark areas so the final paint will show light and dark areas.

computer Lenni lays out the Norm's letters free hand following another set of guide lines marked on the door. Next Lenni uses transfer paper to pick up the Tire Sales lettering off the backing of the Gerber paper and lays it down on the door. Before he starts painting by hand Lenni uses a ruler to be sure the layout is in the same position on each door.

The letters are painted with a lettering brush, a number 10 Raphael manufactured by Chromatic paints. The Norm's letters are done with sign painter's enamel in a process blue color lightened with white. Lenni thins the paint so it brushes on nice and even and doesn't run or leave dry spots: about 5 parts paint to 2 or 3 parts thinner (mineral spirits in this case). For airbrush work he likes it closer to a 2 to 1 ratio.

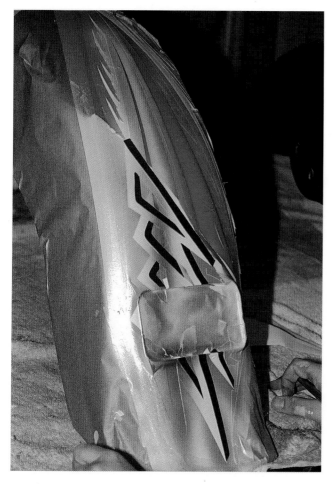

At this point you can see the purple, added to the upper fender, and the basecoats being applied to the inner and upper parts of the triangles.

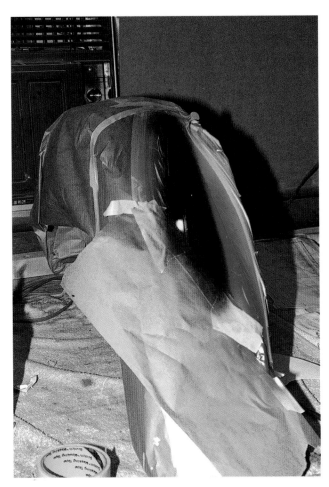

After finishing the triangles Nancy sprays black on the central spear - which is actually the base for the textured area.

After taping off areas around the lettering to minimize overspray it's time to airbrush purple highlights onto the letters with more of the sign painter's enamel. The airbrush is an Iwata Eclipse gun with two stage trigger powered off the shop's air lines. Even though he uses a "cheater" valve on the hose, the high pressure means that when he first pulls the trigger Lenni often gets too much air and paint.

Lenni goes over the purple with a darker blue at the edge of the purple as a transition to the shadow or roll, which is done to add more depth and make a more realistic roll. Now Lenni does a series of white highlights with the airbrush using straight white paint, explaining as he goes that part of the job is figuring out the light source. "In this case the light is coming from over my left shoulder, as I face the job the highlights are on the upper left with shadows on the lower right." Note: the highlights on the right door weren't added until later in the job.

After the Norm's lettering is done and outlined by hand in deep blue Lenni tapes off a horizontal spear under the Norm's lettering. Lenni explains that the idea here is to, "eliminate what's called a 'hot spot.' I try to avoid having a big area of nothing between two areas of type, it makes the type look too far apart, the gray stripe will make it look closer together, makes a better overall design."

The Tires Sales lettering is done by brush in a medium purple color. Lenni pulls the tape when the paint is still pretty fresh, explaining as he does, "if it dries too much before the tape is pulled you get a sharp edge that someone will catch during a wash job and then a corner of the lettering will flake off."

Nancy uses plastic wrap and silver paint to create a textured pattern.

Now Lenni adds a stripe in a coral color below the lettering and a small dingbat in fuscia between the words Tires, and Sales, both of which contribute to the overall design.

The lettering for Little Canada is done essentially freehand, but first Lenni lays out two parallel guide lines and then writes out the letting with a Stabilo pencil. Now he can follow that lettering in lightened process blue, with a number 3 lettering brush, a slightly stiffer brush than a true lettering quill.

It's time now to do the upper pinstripes. The top one, the larger of the two, will be done in a fading pattern. Lenni marks off the places where the color will shift with small pieces of tape.

Starting at the front of the truck Lenni works with lightened process blue for the upper stripe,

Before final clear or pinstripes you can see what all the fuss is about. Note the incredible detail and the amount of work that went into each small part of the design.

then mixes in some darker blue and paints the second color area in the middle of the upper stripe. In a similar fashion he creates an even darker blue for the third color used at the tail-end of the stripe. A small sponge is used to create the blended areas where the color changes.

The last thing is the application of the coral pinstripe, under the blue stripe, and then the addition of the small oscilloscope pattern in fuscia. The end product is a nice clean design done by utilizing a variety of colors, lettering styles and application techniques.

SEQUENCE NUMBER FOUR:

Bruce and John from Wizard Custom Studios put scallops on the big Dodge.

The project shown here is a set of scallops applied to a late model Dodge truck belonging to John

The textured area takes on more character with the addition of some teal color.

This section of lettering was cut out ahead of time, based on known dimensions for the truck door. Transfer paper is used as an aid in positioning the letters on the door.

Sign painter's enamel and a number 10 lettering brush are used to hand letter this part of the design.

Peterson. The job is straightforward and done without painting the entire truck, what you might call an easy way to "wake up" the vehicle. As Bruce Bush, owner of the Wizard shop, explains: "These scallops are a nice simple design, this is the kind of thing that a lot of people could do at home in their own garage." Though the design is relatively simple some of the methods are interesting. Note the use of Marblizer and the way Bruce creates the pinstripe at the beginning of the project.

Bruce and the crew start the job by taking off the obvious things like the antenna and the Ram emblem on the door. He recommends that they leave the door side trim in place because it's an expensive piece of trim if you damage it and also because it's simply easier this way.

As a first step Bruce wipes the front of the truck down

Highlights are added to the hand lettered part of the sign with the airbrush.

Purple and darker blue are added to the letters to give them more depth and create a rolled effect.

A mixed media event, Lenni reverts to the lettering brush to do the outline in deep blue.

The horizontal spear is done by hand in a gray color. The spear is an important part of the overall design and helps to hold all the type together.

Here Lenni pulls the masking after painting in the Tire Sales letters.

with wax and grease remover then the boys scuff the front of the truck with a grey Scotch brite pad. Next they mask off everything that won't be painted. Bruce uses plastic fine line tape at the edge where the grey meets the blue, though any of the thin plastic tapes would have worked there. At the door jamb Bruce tapes the inner edge of the door after wiping the door jamb with a damp cloth. Bruce explains that he actually tapes both the inner door and inner door jamb, "for two reasons: so the paint doesn't get in there but also so when I'm spraying the dust doesn't blow out of that area to get on the rest of the paint job."

Bruce uses conventional 3/4 inch tape up to and half way across the fine line tape, then masking paper for the rest of the job. "I try to mask up all the seams I can and any overlaps in the masking paper," explains the Wizard. "Because either the paint will find it's way under the paper, or the seam holds dust which ends up getting in the paint."

Before doing the layout Bruce takes a tack rag and goes over the entire vehicle. The layout is done freehand with Scotch 1/8 inch blue plastic tape. "Sometimes it's easier to do a simple job like this one without a sketch," explains Bruce. "The sketch doesn't always show body lines, doing it freehand allows me more freedom to change the design half way through if it just doesn't fit the vehicle."

The dingbat is another of those small graphic elements that adds to the design and helps to pull all the type together into one sign.

Once the truck is completely taped off you can really see the shape of the scallops. During the taping Bruce is careful to keep his hands very clean, often taking a minute to wash them. After all the taping is done John goes over the truck lightly with wax and grease remover to eliminate any obvious fingerprints, but also being careful that none of the cleaner gets under the edges of the tape. The final step before beginning to paint is to wipe the area to be painted with a tack rag.

Before hand lettering this part of the sign, Lenni wrote out the letters in Stabilo pencil.

Now Bruce mixes up the purple that will be used for the pinstripe. Bruce sprays this pinstripe color first along the inside of the masked area without further masking, because the scallop color that comes next will cover the purple just fine. The purple lavender from PPG (part of their DBU basecoat series) is applied in two light coats, one shortly after the other. The idea is to get good coverage but without creating too thick a paint film which makes for a big paint edge. Bruce judges the coverage by watching the color of the tape, "I know I've got good coverage when I can't see the colors of the tape at the edge."

After the purple is dry Bruce goes in and lays in 1/8 inch blue tape at the very inside edge of the scallops. Thus the "pinstripe" is already done and exists under this thin tape.

The next step is to run a

The blue pinstripe is done in three slightly different colors with a transition or blended area between each color change.

A sponge is used to dab in the blended areas that separate each color change on the upper pinstripe.

The airbrush and some white paint are used to add the bright highlights to the lettering.

piece of 3/4 inch masking tape from half way across the pinstripe tape to the regular tape. This is done to make sure no paint goes down between the pinstripe tape and the tape used to layout the design.

The next step is the shadow for the scallops done in Camaro, radar purple. Again, Bruce sprays first and does the taping after, because he is going to cover over any overspray anyway. So after the shadow is sprayed Bruce tapes it off with 1/8 blue tape, then covers the whole shadow with 3/4 inch tape. When the shadow is completely covered Bruce mixes up the charcoal, a 1988 Chevy truck color, tacks off the scalloped area and applies two coats of the DBU charcoal paint.

The charcoal dries quickly and soon Bruce is ready to apply the Marblizer. Though the rule of thumb is to never mix paints from two different systems, in this situation Bruce chose to use House of Kolor Marblizer and final clearcoat over the PPG materials sprayed earlier. The Marblizer is a mix of MB-05 lilac-lilac with MB-01 silver-white, mixed half and half.

Bruce and John work as a team. Bruce sprays a roughly rectangular area with the Marblizer and then they put on the saran wrap, which was cut ahead of time. Immediately they move to another area, spray that, apply more wrap and then go back to the first area and pull the wrap. Bruce says he gets the best results by

Lenni Schwartz and the completed sign. What looks like a simple sign project is actually quite complex, when executed by someone who can master both airbrush work and hand lettering.

Here you see Bruce as he begins taping out the scallops freehand across the door of the Dodge. Plastic 3M tape is the material of choice here.

The rest of the masking is done with 3/4 inch masking tape, which is run half way over the plastic tape. At this point it's easy to see what the scallops will really look like - and easy to change as well.

Before spraying Bruce goes over the sheet metal with a tack rag one more time, using caution not to lift the edge of the tape.

This is the pinstripe color being applied at the inside edge of the scallops.

leaving the plastic wrap on about one minute (the tech sheets list a time of five to ten minutes before the wrap is pulled off), "If you pull it too soon the Marblizer is still flowing and you loose the crisp details. if you wait too long it's hard to get the paper off."

The texture of the Marblized area can be altered slightly after the plastic wrap is pulled off by bunching up the wrap and dabbing it against the paint. The actual marble pattern is infinitely variable and depends on how you apply the paint, the paper wrap and when you pull it off. Creative types sometimes use bubble-pack wrap or something other than regular plastic wrap to achieve a more interesting or unique pattern. After Bruce is happy with the Marblized effect on the front of the truck he spays on one coat of SG-100 before pulling all the tape.

"I like to pull the tape as quickly as I can. You've got a window of time in terms of when the clear needs to go on, and you're less likely to pull paint if you pull the tape right away." The final clearcoat is made up of four medium coats of UC-1, allowing for flash times between each coat.

Sequence number five: Tri-colored tanks, painted by Jon Kosmoski.

The Harley-Davidson tanks seen in this sequence were painted in my personal shop. Though at first they seem like a simple project, blending colors, especially pearls, is anything but simple.

More fine line tape is used at the inside edge of the scallops to cover what will be the "pinstripe."

Before starting on the project I did some test panels for the customer so I would be sure to give them exactly the colors they were looking for. Prepping and painting the test panels took me an extra four hours, time that I couldn't charge the customer for - but painting the panels and showing them to the customer meant I was sure to give them what they wanted. Time spent doing test panels must to be built into the price of the overall job.

After prepping the tanks as you would any sheet metal, I applied two coats of the white base, BC-26. Actually, for a light pearl color you could use a grey base, because the grey will add more depth to the pearl. In this case the customer wants the paint really bright so I'm using a white base under white pearl.

The design calls for a three color blend and after the white base has flashed I apply three coats of PC-6 violet pearl. The PC-6 is mixed with RU-310 reducer (our fastest), even though it's almost 80 degrees in the shop. This way the material dries faster and I can come in with the next coat quickly. If I was applying the final clear I might use 311 or a mix or 311 and 310 because that way the paint flows longer and you get more "leveling" time. Even though the material is drying quickly I am careful to make sure it has flashed (dry to the touch, not the least bit sticky) before putting on another coat

The "pinstripe" tape is bridged with conventional masking tape so no paint can get down into the seam between the layout and the pinstripe tape.

The shadow for the scallops is done in a fashion similar to the way the pinstripe was done - by spraying the color first and masking it off later.

Here you can see how the shadow color is already applied and taped over - at the edge, first with blue plastic tape and then with conventional masking tape.

109

Now it's time to apply the first coat of charcoal paint, which will be allowed to dry before applying a second coat.

Application of the Marblizer is next. Bruce applied the special material to one small area, then applies the plastic wrap and moves on to spray another.

so I'm sure not to trap any solvents. Some guys put the paint on so fast they do trap solvents and that creates problems for them down the road because the trapped solvents will try to work their way out of the film and dull the paint job when they do.

This blend job goes from light to medium to dark. I apply three coats of PC-6 first, two-thirds of the way up the parts. In this case the light violet will act as a base for the medium tone and help make a smooth blend. The medium color is PBC-39 hot pink pearl.

There are a few tricks to doing smooth blends with these pearls. It helps to use a good gun with great atomization. For this job I'm

Following the application of the Marblizer Bruce and John put the plastic wrap up against the still-wet paint and then wait a few minutes before removing the wrap.

using a GEO HVLP gun because it has a really fine, even atomization pattern. And in order to avoid blotchiness when doing blends with pearls I move in close and use a limited trigger pull on the gun.

Each color of PBC is one "coat", but I do it in multiple, almost dry, passes. I just put the pearl on until I get the coverage that I want. Once I switch to the darker color I start spraying at the back of the tank (the darker end). I use wrist action and turn the gun toward the center of the tank. As I get it pointed toward the center part, where it blends to the lighter color, I let up on the trigger so by the time the gun is pointing toward the blended area I'm only spraying air not paint. This requires practice, the air blows away the overspray and improves the blend. This same practice is common to spot repair work.

In order to apply the paint evenly to the parts

On the right, you can see that as the plastic wrap is pulled off, a unique marble-like pattern is left behind. If you look at the photo of the hood you can see that it isn't uniform but changes slightly over the surface.

The final shot - certainly a wake-up call for an otherwise plain vehicle and all done without removing the factory paint.

The PC-6 violet pearl is sprayed over a white base which leaves it looking very light in color.

Here we come in with the hot pink, applied with a gravity-feed HVLP gun. You have to have a mental picture of the part so you know how far to go with each color.

on either side of the bike you have to make a mental picture of where you're starting the new color and then keep that in your head as you work on the job. After the final darkest pearl is applied, and has flashed, you can't do anything to it, don't tack it or anything, just let it dry and then go in with the clears.

With regard to the clearcoats, you have to remember that the clear won't hide anything so you have to do it right. The first coat should be a light "bond" coat followed by two heavier, wetter coats. For the last coat I like to strain it really carefully as I mix the materials. It's a good idea to use a fine mesh screen, 190 microns, and put two Kimwipes in the bottom, that way you don't have any seeds from the catalyst or impurities that might leave lumps in your paint.

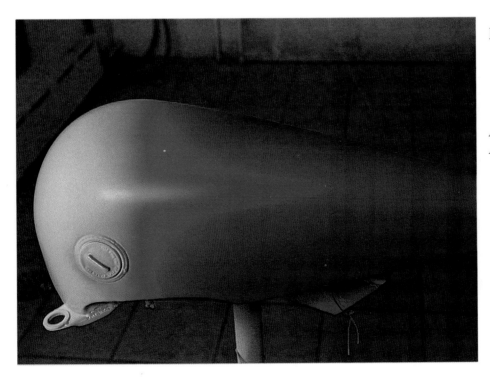

The hot pink is applied to two-thirds of the tank in a series of passes done with a limited trigger pull.

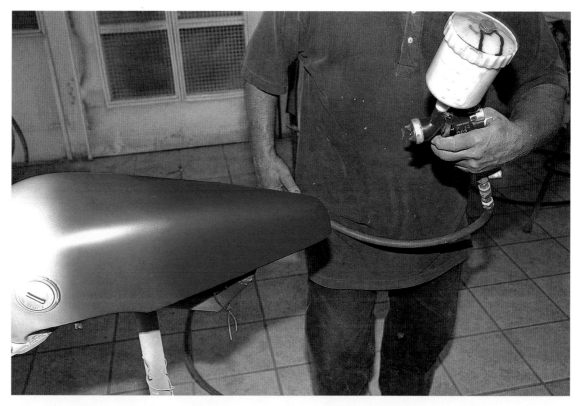

When doing the darkest color I start at the back of the tank and turn the gun toward the front, letting up on the trigger as I do.

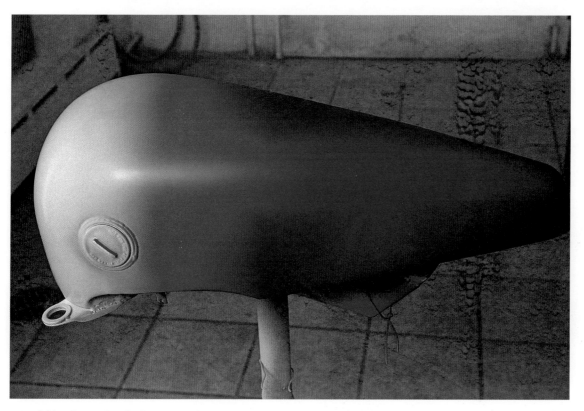

Good blends can be challenging. They require a good spray gun, and practice with the application techniques outlined in the text.

Chapter Seven

Hands On

A Four-wheel Graphic, A Two-wheeled Paint Job.

This second of the Hands-On chapters documents two start-to-finish graphics jobs. One is a fairly complex multi-layer job done on a late model Chevy Tahoe. The second sequence is a very elaborate job done on a motorcycle. In this second case

the graphics *are* the paint job.

For both jobs the first step is a rendering or detailed sketch, followed by multiple masking and painting operations before the job is finished. So follow along as two very different jobs move

This is the finished product, the Chevy Tahoe with graphics created by Let's Get Graphic. For more on   *how these special effects were created, read on...*

114

through two shops at the hands of three artists - all of whom have something to say about this graphics business.

SEQUENCE NUMBER ONE:

Brian Gall and Leah Begin from Let's Get Graphic.

Brian Gall went to school to be a body man and that might be his current trade, except for one incident. "In school I could do the body work pretty well," recalls Brian. "But one day I did a set of flames on a hood and they turned out pretty well so I just started to do more and more of that type of work.

Since opening Let's Get Graphic in 1990 Brian has added two very valuable members to the crew: Leah Begin who does all their airbrushing, and Lenni Hubbard who came to the shop with a background in computer-generated graphics and sign work.

The work seen here is done on a 1997 Chevy Tahoe. Before starting the job Brian and Leah worked up a rendering of the finished vehicle and used that to get the customer's approval.

Brian starts by scuffing the sides of the new Chevy with 400 grit sand paper on the DA sander, then applies two coats of DP-90 epoxy primer from PPG. Next comes two coats of teal from PPG (this is code 42, a 1994 Chevy color) applied with a new DeVilbiss OMX, HVLP gun running on 45 psi. Brian applies 2 medium coats of the teal to get good coverage.

Brian explains that he likes to work backwards, "I like to paint an area, mask it off and then paint the next layer." Next Leah and Brian apply the first piece of Gerber masking vinyl so Leah can draw out the ripped upper edge of the checkerboard section. She draws out both sides of the upper rip with Stabilo pencil and then gets ready to cut along the line with an X-Acto knife.

"The key to cutting the vinyl on the car or truck," says Leah, "is to only cut once so you don't have to go back over it, this is much easier with a very sharp X-Acto blade. Sometimes the left-over piece you remove can be used someplace else on the truck, just so it isn't too beat up and will still stick to the truck with good adhesion."

After cutting out the top rip, the one that runs along the upper edge of the design, they do the lower border for the checkerboard pattern. For rips

Brian likes to work from a sketch, so both he and the customer know what the final job is going to look like.

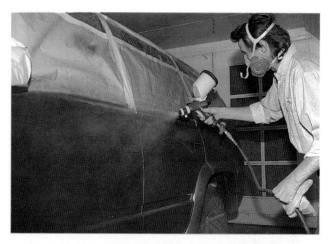

Brian uses an HVLP gun from DeVilbiss to apply two coats of teal paint.

You can see the vinyl "stripe" running diagonally across the body panels as Leah draws out the ripped line that will form the upper border.

The vinyl is cut with, "a very sharp" X-Acto knife according to the lines drawn earlier.

The two pieces of ripped vinyl, which converge near the back of the truck, will mask the checkerboard area.

Next comes vinyl masking material for the large islands of purple in the center of the design.

and complex patterns she and Brian agree that you can get a much cleaner pattern with sharp "tears" by using a pattern cut from vinyl than you can with any kind of masking tape. After all the small rips are done Brian and Leah put on a large piece of Gerber masking paper on the left side of the truck and Leah draws out more rips and tears. Before firing up the spray gun Brian takes up a gun of a different sort, a heat gun which is used to soften the vinyl so it can be pushed down into the body creases and seams. Masking tape is used to bridge any tears or breaks in the vinyl.

Next Brian sprays the purple into the middle of the large ripped areas in the center of the doors and panels. The purple is Shimrin PBC-40 from House of Kolor, mixed to standard ratios, applied in 3 medium coats to get good coverage. Brian waits 15 minutes between coats, (though this depends on the temperature). He and Leah now spray the shadow on the upper part of the purple area. This shadow is done with a special mix made up of black mixed with purple. Leah explains that, "Mixing the purple with black will give a softer more realistic shadow than just black alone." Leah does her shadows according to an imaginary light source, "You have to know where the light is coming from, then you can figure out where the shadows should be."

The conventional siphon-style spray gun, a Binks No 7, is adjusted to a dot pattern by eliminating any air to the "horns" and leaving the material knob at the standard setting. The paint is applied in a series of passes until Brian likes the look of the shadow. Intercoat clear is applied to the shadow and purple areas because these will be taped off before any more painting is done and the clear will protect the paint from any tape marks.

The checkerboard area is next, Brian starts by spraying three coats of BC-25 black, with 15 minute flash times between each coat, across the entire area. He does the black first because it is easier to touch up later if there is a mis-tape. Over the black he applies intercoat clear SG-100. When the intercoat is dry he and Leah put Gerbermask over the area that was sprayed with black.

At this point Leah draws out the checkerboard pattern freehand on the vinyl before removing every other square. Looking at the checkerboard before the painting - the white areas represent the tape and the black areas are the places where there is no tape. The pattern at this point is in fact an exact reverse of the finished job after painting.

Before spraying the white Brain goes over all the tape edges to be sure they are adhering to the surface and no paint will migrate under the edges of the vinyl. When tacking an area like this one it's important to tack gently so as not to lift the edges or corners of the masking material.

With the checkerboard painted white and then taped over, the entire side of the car is painted with two coats of a medium gray. Then Leah comes back and applies the darker waves on the gray. The first of the darker lines are applied with the air brush in a random pattern, very much by hand. After painting on the first set of flowing lines Leah mixes a lighter gray and applies that essentially over the first set of lines.

The last thing they do that is really part of the design is to mix a dark gray and use that to darken (create a shadow) under the purple splashes. Before they are completely finished with the whole thing, after Brian has un-taped most of the left side, Leah adds shadows which give depth to the white edge of the checkerboard banner.

Now it's time to pull any remaining vinyl and go around to double check the vehicle for mis-tapes or mistakes that need to be touched up.

SEQUENCE NUMBER TWO:

Andy Anderson, Anderson Studios Inc., Nashville, Tennessee

These photos document part of the elaborate paint job Andy Anderson performed on a certain very custom Harley-Davidson that he built for himself. Andy is knowledgeable in more than one field, as Anderson Studios is also a very high quality screen printing facility. But Andy loves motorcycles almost as much as he loves painting. In fact, his first paint job was done with spray cans when he was about 15 years old. At age 17 Andy built his first Harley and says that custom painting motorcycles, "is still my first love."

No matter how busy the T-shirt business gets there's always at least one custom bike in the basement of the building. On weekends when he isn't printing beautiful full color T-shirts Andy is in the paint booth working on a personal project or a bike belonging to a select group of customers. Past customers include well-known

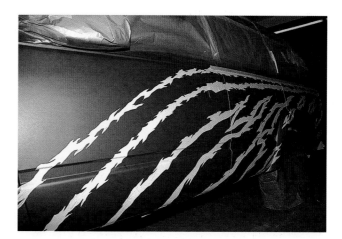

Other than making sure the vinyl is stuck to the car, and a final tacking, this side of the truck is ready for the next step in the painting sequence.

The same HVLP gun seen earlier is used to apply purple to the masked areas in the center of the panels.

Following the application of the purple, a purple and black mix is used to create the shadowed areas. Before being taped these areas will get a coat of SG-100.

117

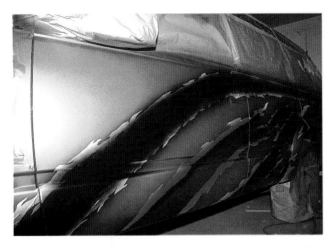

When the purple areas are finished it's time to apply the black to the checkerboard area.

Now they apply vinyl to the checkerboard area and draw out the squares before doing any cutting.

Every other square is cut out with an X-Acto knife. The next step is the application of the white paint.

artists like Jimmy Buffet, Barbara Mandrell and Neil Young, all of whom had Andy do the murals on their tour buses.

Andy has more than just personal drive going for him when he takes on a painting project. Between that first "spray bomb" paint job and the establishment of Anderson Studios as a viable custom painting and screen printing shop Andy went to art school. That fine-art background means Andy has a thorough understanding of color theory, parts of which come through in the following explanations of how he painted the custom Softail Harley-Davidson seen here. Andy took all the photos and sent elaborate notes along with the film so we just left the story in Andy's words - straight from the painter's mouth so to speak. And because the job is so elaborate the copy and photos only deal with the majority of the graphics applied to the gas tank and side panels.

To begin with all items are prepared using the best filler, primer and primer surfacer, like KP-2 Kwikure epoxy from House of Kolor. The tank and side covers start out being painted with Shimrin base coats, a mixture of lemon yellow SG-101 and chrome yellow SG-102, sprayed over a white base BC-26. Then I came over the top of that with Inca gold pearl (a dry pearl), mixed with SG-100. I like to use SG-100 in these situations because it allows me to get a more even coating. I can spray and blend it with more flexibility, the window of time during which I can add more topcoats is longer than it would be with a topcoat-type clear. This helps produce a nice even pearl coat. If, for example, I use UC-1 (urethane topcoat clear) with the dry pearl then three or four coats creates a much thicker film.

Once the base coats are finished I put 4 coats of UC-1 over everything, let it sit at least 12 hours and sand it with 400 grit wet sandpaper. If someone is inexperienced I tell them to use 500 grit because it doesn't sand through too quickly, otherwise I use 400 grit. This surface will provide good adhesion for the graphics that will follow, it creates good "tooth" for the next coats of paint.

I do a sketch of the layout first, then the actual layout with 1/8 or 1/6th inch fine-line tape. Once I've laid out the design I mask off the total area that won't be painted with graphics. Next I cut out all my "over and unders" so I get basecoat on all the

After masking the checkerboard and purple areas a medium grey is applied to the side and back of the Tahoe.

graphic areas. Then comes the orion silver BC-02, enough coats to provide good coverage. I like the medium size flake in this paint, it works well under the kandies that will follow and gives them good depth.

Now I apply SG-100 , 2 coats, to protect everything. I let that dry a minimum of one hour (depending on shop conditions) before doing any taping. It's a good idea to check this clear before starting to tape on it, by putting a piece of tape in a non-critical area and waiting a few minutes to see if it will leave an imprint. If it hasn't you can proceed with the taping and graphics. If the SG-100 sits over night it should be sanded with 500 or 600 grit sand paper, but you must be careful as this is a non-catalyzed paint and it's pretty thin. This is more work perhaps but has the advantage of eliminating any dust nibs in the paint.

Before applying the graphic colors I determine exactly which colors go where. I do that with a colored sketch or rendering. The rendering has the advantage that now everybody knows what the finished job will look like. It's a good tool to show the customer and also a good road map for anyone working with me in the shop.

I like to do the dominant part of the design first. This one had 2 dominant areas, the purple ovals and the magenta spears. We started with the magenta areas which were sprayed with magenta kandy koncentrate mixed with SG-100 (I often mix my own kandy-colors this way). The coverage isn't always the same, there's a fade toward the rear of the spear for example. The lighter and darker areas add depth, I sometimes do that with color intensity. I want to show the illusion of some sort of dimension or form.

At the front area of the stripe where it comes up from the lower part of the tank I came in and did Marblizer, but in a subtle fashion. I did this on top of the magenta with purple candy toner and blue-pink Marblizer MB-04, applied over the purple candy toner. I used plastic wrap to get the effect I wanted. From there I cleared each graphic with SG 100.

Now I went to my purple areas, the purple arches and the spear on the tank. They are done

A contrasting light grey is the next color to be applied. Again, the paint is applied free-hand with the airbrush (a relatively large jar is attached to the bottom of the airbrush).

Here you can see how both the dark and light streaks are run right over the masked areas, and how the lines diverge at the center of the door.

with purple and magenta koncentrates (KK-10 and KK-16 respectively). I created a series of blends with the two colors. This was done with two airbrushes set up ahead of time with the two colors. The highlight seen at the front of the arch is just the basecoat silver showing through. The deeper purple streak has silver Marblizer over it with candy toner over that to tint it.

For the marbled orange areas in the center of the tank I mixed my own kandy with koncentrate and SG-100, with tangerines and some reds. After spraying you can dab it with a sponge or saran wrap - that's how I got the textured orange areas in the middle of the tank. I wanted a textured effect with kandy colors and there's no real definitive way to do that. I spent time with test panels before starting in on the actual sheet metal.

The next step is to reverse tape again to do the top orange and the white fade. The top orange is tangerine kandy koncentrate mixed to the preferred strength and faded out from the graphics. I streaked it with kandy magenta and highlighted with tinted white for effect.

When all of the graphics are done I cleared the graphics areas with UC-1 I apply the UC-1 with a touch up gun only to the areas with graphics. I apply 3 or 4 coats, allowing for flash time between coats. By doing it this way I don't get too many layers of clear on the whole

Here you see the shadows being added under the checkerboard area and the purple splashes.

All the steps, the colors and shadows and contrasting lines across the body, come together here. This job requires the imagination to conceive the design, the ability to determine the sequence, and the skill to actually apply the paint.

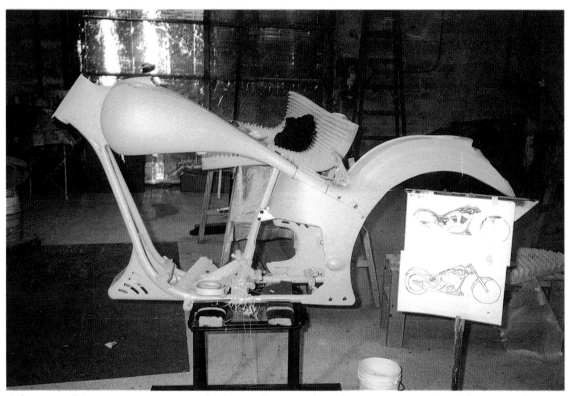

This is Andy's painting project as the layout begins. The yellow is a mix of two Shimrin colors, topcoated with Inca gold pearl. Note the sketches kept nearby for reference. Andy keeps a detailed photo record of all the work that goes through the shop. Andy Anderson

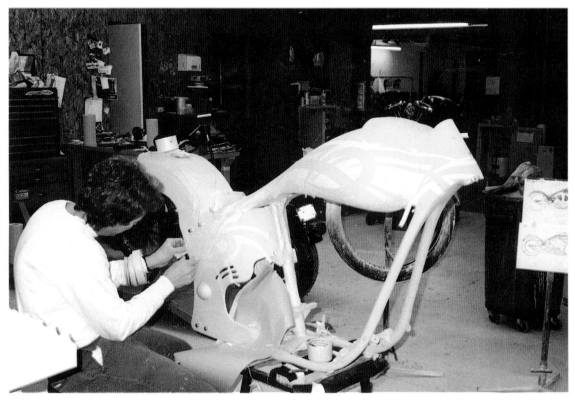

The original layout is done with plastic tape, before all the other areas are masked off. The next step will be application of three coats of orion silver used as a base under all the graphic areas. Andy Anderson

bike. I let the clear dry overnight, 12 hours minimum. Then I'm ready for wet sanding. I sand edges down to where they're almost invisible. On the first layers of clear you need to use caution, you don't want to sand into your graphics.

I mix paint for the pinstripes to get exactly the right colors. I like to use Urethane Striping Enamel. The idea is to make the designs themselves stand out. Striping makes the colors stand out which really adds to the design. It also gives it that finished detail touch. There are six different colors of stripes in this job.

The process blue and green are wider stripes, I taped them off and sprayed them, but the others are done in a conventional fashion with a brush. The green is bold and adds more visual pizzazz and compliments the oranges. Against those edges there is a pinstripe too. After the process blue was dry I added the very narrow strip of fuscia with a brush.

The shadowing that I do I like to do right over the pinstripes. The way I do it gives the dimension of depth to the whole design. Even though the pinstriping around the graphics is the "finishing" step, I like to shadow everything, including the pinstripes.

The shadowing can be done with cut or thinned black, or what would be the true shadow color. During my art school days we didn't use black. It's better to use deeper purples and blues to

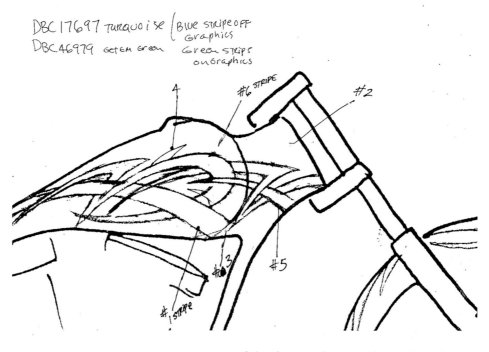

A variety of sketches are done until the design seems right for the bike. Both a black and white sketch like this, showing all the colors, and a color sketch are done before the graphics painting begins.

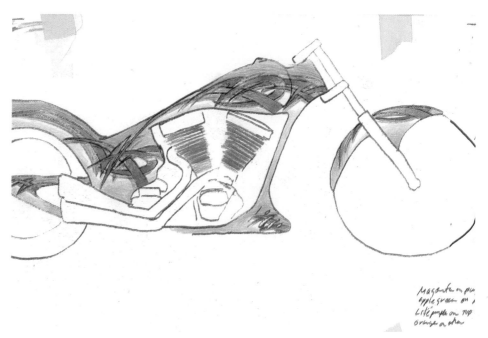

This is the road map of the actual job. Something that will help everyone in the shop keep track of each step during this very complex paint job.

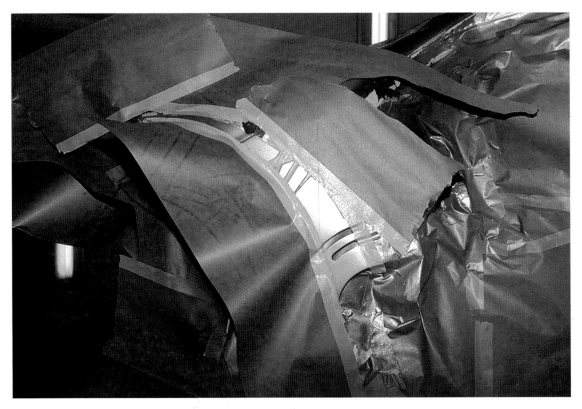

Here we see one spear taped off under the seat, in silver basecoat before application of the kandys and Marblizers that make up this paint job. Andy Anderson

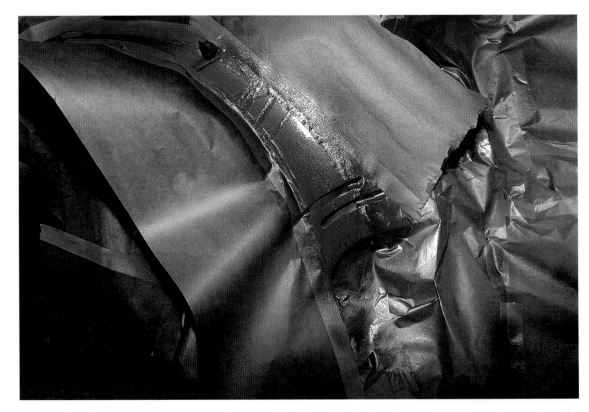

The spears show subtle marblized effects and fading. The basic color and shading is created with purple and magenta kandy colors. A silver marblizer is sprayed over the top and dabbed with plastic wrap to create the texture. Next comes more kandy, mixed from purple and magenta toners, then SG-100. Andy Anderson

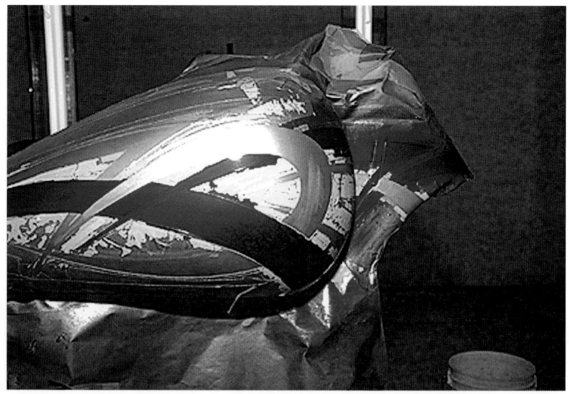

This spear coming up from the lower side of the tank was done in similar fashion. First, create the color and fade with kandys, then apply silver marblizer for subtle effect. Finally, topcoat the marblizer with more kandy mixed from toners. Andy Anderson

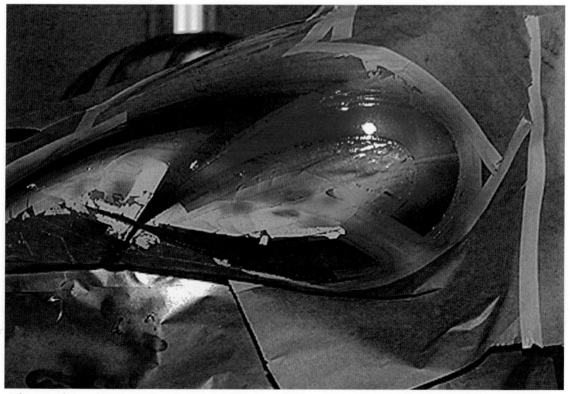

The purple ovals were created with kandy mixed from toners (also called Intensifiers). Purple and magenta were blended to give a more interesting appearance, at the front the paints were applied sparingly so the basecoat silver would show through and create a highlight. A. Anderson

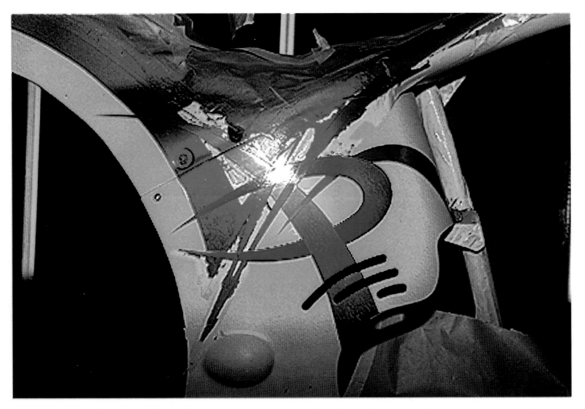

Here you can better see how the lower spear seen earlier fades from purple to magenta. Andy Anderson

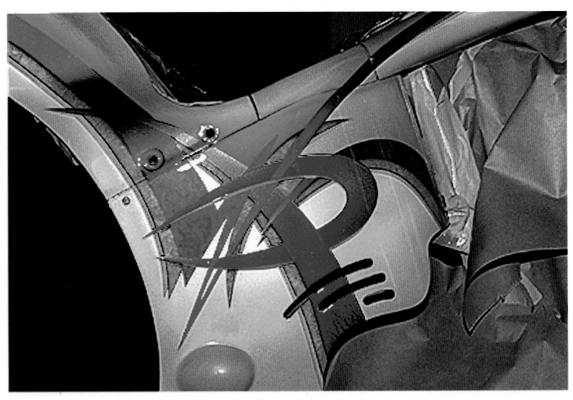

To add more brightness and contrast to the area under the seat a faded silver area was added. Note also the added green and blue pinstriping which was taped off and sprayed. Andy Anderson

create the darker color - you get a clearer, purer color that way. You can also use the compliment of the color being shadowed. Over the white areas I mixed purple and orange to get the grey shadow color.

If you study the masters, the renaissance painters and the impressionists they were true geniuses of color work. If you read about them it's fascinating to learn how they achieved contrast, light and shadow. One thing I learned, they always worked from pure colors and often mixed their own paint from raw pigments. I think one of the most significant things I learned in school was to not use black because it gets muddy. We would work from red, yellow and blue, the primary colors. We had the purest of those colors to work with and we mixed our own colors from those.

The final clearing was three separate steps using three to five coats each time. The goal was to achieve a glass-smooth finish with no paint edges. Sanding between coats was done at this point with 400 grit, working up to 500 grit on the last clearing. Then the job was sanded with 1000/1500/2000 grit and polished to a glass-like finish. I have to add that this is optional. A lot of times your last coat is smooth enough to not have to polish. It's up to you and your customer.

The finished close-up of the gas tank shows the full effect of the pinstripes and the textured areas in the center. Note the incredible detail in the shadows.

A finished side view shows how all the steps, the masking painting and tinting, come together to form one very bright, custom Harley-Davidson.

Sources

Anderson Studios
2609 Grissom Dr
Nashville, TN 37204
615 255 4807
FAX: 615 255 4812

Brooks Signs
74 Industrial Way
Hanover, MA 02339
617 871 6361
FAX 617 871 5144

House of Kolor
Valspar
210 Crosby St.
Picayune MS 39466
800 845 2500
House of Kolor tech line
612 375 8790

Kosmoski Specialties
2519 27th Av. So.
MPLS MN 55406

Krazy Kolors
Attn: Lenni Schwartz
2177 Holloway
No St. Paul, MN 55109
612 777 1124

l.i.n.e.
Rory Bedell
PO Box 19
Greenlawn NY 11740
516 261 9707
516 261 9705

Mack Brushes
Andrew Mack and Son Brush Company
225 E Chicago St.
Jonesville, MI 49250
517 849 9272

Let's Get Graphic
7731 E Hwy 65 Service Dr.
Spring Lake Park, MN 55432
612 783 8119

Jeremy Vecoli
4404 Portland Av S
MPLS, MN 55407
612 825 3113

Paasche Air Brush Co.
7440 W Lawrence Av
Harwood Heights, IL 60656
708 867 9191

Smith, Craig
7015 Portland Av. S.
MPLS, MN 55423
612 798 0640

Wizard Custom Studios
1248 Andover Blvd
Ham Lake, MN 55304
612 413 0048